ROBERT

ELEVATING

EQUITY

AND

JUSTICE

10 U.S. Supreme Court Cases
Every Teacher Should Know

FOREWORD BY
Lily Eskelsen García, PRESIDENT, NEA

HEINEMANN
Portsmouth, NH

Heinemann

361 Hanover Street

Portsmouth, NH 03801–3912

www.heinemann.com

Offices and agents throughout the world

> *Heinemann's authors have devoted their entire careers to developing the unique content in their works, and their written expression is protected by copyright law. We respectfully ask that you do not adapt, reuse, or copy anything on third-party (whether for-profit or not-for-profit) lesson sharing websites.*
>
> **—Heinemann Publishers**

"Dedicated to Teachers" is a trademark of Greenwood Publishing Group, Inc.

The author and publisher wish to thank those who have generously given permission to reprint borrowed images:

Page 4: AP Photo/Ron Edmonds/file; Page 16: © 2018 The Dallas Morning News, Inc.; Page 29: AP Photo/Ted S. Warren; Page 41: Illustration by Vita Lane; Page 53: © Delcia Lopez/San Antonio Express-News/ZUMA Press; Page 65: From San Francisco Public Library; Page 77: Bettmann/Getty Images; Page 89: Pam Parry/Baptist Joint Committee for Religious Liberty, 1991; Page 103: Photo by Mark Wilson/Getty Images; page 115: Illustration by Vita Lane

Library of Congress Cataloging-in-Publication Data

Name: Kim, Robert (Robert J.), author.

Title: Elevating equity and justice: ten U.S. Supreme Court cases every
    teacher should know / Robert Kim.

Description: Portsmouth : Heinemann, 2019. | Includes bibliographical
    references and index.

Identifiers: LCCN 2019031285 | ISBN 9780325092140

Subjects: LCSH: Educational law and legislation—United States—Cases. |
    Constitutional law—United States—Cases. | Teachers—United
    States—Handbooks, manuals, etc.

Classification: LCC KF4119.85 .K56 2019 | DDC 344.73/08—dc23

LC record available at https://lccn.loc.gov/2019031285

Editor: Holly Kim Price

Production Editor: Sonja S. Chapman

Typesetter: Kim Arney

Cover and interior designs: Vita Lane

Manufacturing: Steve Bernier

Printed in the United States of America on acid-free paper

23 22 21 20 19   CGB   1 2 3 4 5

Dedication

For my partner, Mark;
my parents, Theresa and Henry;
and all those who teach, mentor,
or advocate for students

CONTENT

1 **CASE 1** Davis v. Monroe County Board of Education (1999)

Schools are responsible for appropriately addressing sexual harassment and violence among students.

Topic: Sexual Harassment

Main Lesson: Educators must respond appropriately to student-on-student sexual harassment; students have a right to be protected from harassment under Title IX of the Education Amendments of 1972.

14 **CASE 2** Plyler v. Doe (1982)

Schools may not deny school-age children who are undocumented immigrants a free public education.

Topic: Immigrant Students

Main Lesson: Schools must admit (and educators must treat) immigrant students, including undocumented students, equally; undocumented students have a right to equal protection under the Fourteenth Amendment of the U.S. Constitution.

Topic: Equal Educational Opportunity

Main Lesson: A child does not have a federal constitutional right to an education in the United States or a federal right to equitably funded schools; as a result, most school funding challenges now take place in state court, asserting violations of state law.

English learners are entitled to equal educational opportunity and a meaningful education.

Topic: English Learners

Main Lesson: Students with limited English proficiency are entitled to equal educational opportunity and a meaningful education; English learners deserve equal protection under the Fourteenth Amendment of the U.S. Constitution.

Students' free-speech rights must be respected unless the speech substantially interferes with school operations.

Topic: Free Speech

Main Lesson: Students' speech or expression may not be abridged unless it substantially and materially interferes with school operations; students have a First Amendment right of free speech.

Foreword

Whether you're a teacher, administrator, parent, or activist: I know you're busy. I don't care. Put down what you're working on and pick up this book.

I say this to you because everything we hope to accomplish to make our schools gateways to opportunity is in danger. And part of the danger is not knowing all we need to know about the basic legal rights (from the U.S. Supreme Court) of our students and what's happening to erase those rights.

The pillars and pronouncements of the Supreme Court may seem a long way from our classrooms. But they're not. Metaphorically speaking, we're right there, just steps from the highest court in the land. Like a double helix of DNA, the law is closely intertwined with the lives of educators—including my own.

Take *Brown v. Board of Education*. Nearly seventy years ago, Chief Justice Earl Warren wrote, "in the field of public education, the doctrine of separate but equal has no place." With this sentence, the Supreme Court confirmed once and for all that all students, no matter their race, had a right to an equal education under a shared roof.

These words changed the course of history and opened the door of opportunity to generations of students of color. They also enabled me, a Latina woman, to become a teacher in a classroom with students of many races and eventually a leader of the largest labor union in the United States.

It's no coincidence that many of our nation's most iconic court cases involve schools. After all, equal opportunity is one of this country's most cherished founding principles. It follows that instilling equal and basic rights in education is essential to our democracy. Children not only need to learn about equal educational opportunity, they need to *experience* it.

In fact, I've often thought—along with pedagogy for reading, writing, and 'rithmetic—that all aspiring teachers should have classes in the basic legal rights of students and the responsibilities of educators and school systems to protect those rights.

Our responsibility as educators, however, goes beyond simply knowing about and respecting students' rights. As they say, knowledge equals power. To read about the landmark Supreme Court cases involving education and civil rights is to be reminded of the chasm between courts and classrooms, between principles and practice, and between rhetoric and reality.

We have seen what fulfilling the promise of *Brown* looks like through the successes of students, yet, for too many children across the country, the promise of *Brown* is still just that—a promise. Students read about *Brown v. Board of Education* in their history books but often do not see its impact in the world around them.

As I ponder several of the perfectly selected cases in the pages of *Elevating Equity and Justice*, I find myself coming back to the same questions: What happened to *Brown*? Where are the principles Justice Warren articulated back in 1954? Where are they in the 2007 case *Parents Involved in Community Schools* (see page 26), in which the Supreme Court held that public schools were *constitutionally* prohibited from taking certain steps to consider race as a factor in assigning students to school, even if a school district wished to make up for past discrimination against people of color?

As we witness the separation of undocumented parents and their children and the deportation of thousands of immigrants, what remains of the spirit of *Brown* and the 1982 case *Plyler v. Doe* (see page 14), in which the Supreme Court said that schools cannot constitutionally deny students a free public education based on their immigration status?

And how meaningful is *Brown*'s concept of educational equality after *San Antonio v. Rodriguez* (see page 50), the 1973 case in which the Supreme Court astonishingly told us that, while "the grave significance of education both to the individual and to our society cannot be doubted . . . education, of course, is not among the rights afforded explicit protection under our Federal Constitution . . . nor do we find any basis for saying it is implicitly so protected"? Pause a moment to let that sink in. The Court is telling poor children and children of color that, in effect, they have to fend for themselves, that their Constitution cannot help them, and that their government gives thousands of fewer dollars per pupil to the government-funded schools they attend than it provides for schools attended by wealthy, white children.

The inescapable truth is the equality and inclusion that *Brown* was meant to guarantee is not the current reality for our children. There are nearly 51 million children in public schools across the United States. For them, we must recognize that *Brown* is not a self-fulfilling promise—it is one that requires action each and every day. Education has to work for everyone, or it does not work for anyone.

By responding to the continuing inequity and injustice in our schools, Bob Kim's *Elevating Equity and Justice* represents both a useful tool and a call to action. It recognizes that as educators with caring and committed dedication to our students, we have the unique power, ability, and responsibility to increase equity and justice in education and, in doing so, strengthen and preserve our democracy.

The cases and topics explored in these pages cover the landscape of civil rights and civil liberties in K–12 education and are especially relevant today as we struggle through an era in which they are front and center in our national and local headlines. I appreciate how Bob describes these ten blockbuster cases in an accessible way for busy teachers, and that he includes the voices and perspectives of actual school practitioners, who bring to life the connection between the law and the classroom.

Best of all, *Elevating Equity and Justice* reminds us that advancing equality and freedom is *within our power*. It's not just about changing laws or policies or eradicating centuries of discrimination or oppression (although that would certainly help). It's about how we treat our students, how we structure our lessons, what we encourage in discussions, and what we stand up for at school. We can do this.

If each of us is inspired by even one of the cases described in the pages that follow to take one positive action on behalf of a single student, then we will have collectively formed a new civil rights movement affecting millions. Now *that's* exciting!

—Lily Eskelsen García
President, National Education Association

Acknowledgments

My inspiration to write this book arose out of a lifelong commitment to securing greater equity and justice for students in the United States. This commitment has been nurtured and fueled by countless interactions with teachers, professors, mentors, colleagues, advocates, clients, students, and friends. I thank them all for their wisdom and support. In particular, I thank the late Stuart Biegel, whose generosity and spirit I will hold close always.

I am indebted to the following educators who provided smart and insightful perspectives and advice for this book, including Alex Corbitt, Tricia Ebarvia, Tanya Green, Julie Jee, Liz Kleinrock, Kim Parker, Kara Pranikoff, Jamaica Ross, and others who preferred to remain anonymous but whose contributions were no less valuable.

I am also grateful for the amazing people at Heinemann Publishing who helped to bring this book into the world, including Steve Bernier, Sonja Chapman, Vita Lane, Krysten Lebel, Elizabeth Silvis, Brett Whitmarsh, and Lynette Winegarner.

I owe a special debt of gratitude to my dear friend and editor at Heinemann, Holly Price, whose constant encouragement, nudging, prodding, poking, and occasional food and shelter got me through the finish line.

Finally, big hugs to some VIPs in my life who have been constants during a period of flux when this book was written: Ayumi, Yuuki, Elaine, Luna, and, especially, Mark.

Introduction

Say you're a teacher in a public school district. One day, as you begin a lesson, a student starts making loud guttural noises. You ask him to stop, but he keeps making the noises. The other students start laughing and imitating the student. You consider sending the student to the vice principal's office, but then you remember that the student suffers from a behavioral disorder and has an IEP (a individual education plan). You quickly distribute a class assignment you'd been saving for later in the week and then counsel the disruptive student in the hallway.

The next day, during science class, a different student tells you that the upcoming reading on the evolution of the skulls from reptile to amphibian to mammal violates his religion as a Jehovah's Witness. When you tell him he has to complete the reading and related assignment or receive an unsatisfactory grade, he says that you are violating his right to free exercise of his religion.

On day three, a Muslim student who is an immigrant to the United States confides in you that she (along with other Muslim and immigrant students) are being bullied at her bus stop and in the cafeteria. You wonder how you might support this student and other victims of bullying—and whether you have an obligation to report the conversation, even though you were asked to keep it a secret.

The preceding vignettes are fictional. But they are similar to very real situations that occur in schools every day. If you've taught in a K–12 setting, chances are you've had at least one similar experience. In one sense, these episodes depict the familiar challenge of student and classroom management. But they also raise several important topics with a legal dimension: Disability rights. Bullying and harassment. Free exercise of religion. Discrimination. These are, in fact, legal issues that swirl constantly around millions of teachers, administrators, and school personnel.

As an education policy expert and former civil rights lawyer, I have spent much of the last two decades focused on the rights of students as well as the legal rights and obligations of schools and educators. I've advocated for students who were discriminated against as well as for teachers who faced legal problems with their district. I've worked as a legal and policy trainer for teachers and school districts. I've served in a federal education civil rights office that receives and investigates thousands of school-related civil rights complaints annually from people all over the United States. And I've co-written two books on legal issues in education. Over time, I've developed a sense of what legal issues tend to come up for educators, as well as what educators need to know to navigate those issues. And yet, I'm still learning. If there's one true thing about schools, it's that there's never a dull moment; there's always a new challenge or controversy. So for me, there's never a dull legal or policy moment. (Okay, maybe one or two—but rarely, I swear.)

The connection between cases written by judges and the business of teaching may not seem obvious. Isn't legal compliance the exclusive province of the school district lawyer, the board, or an administrator? In fact, educators act in ways, whether consciously or unconsciously, that have legal implications on a daily basis. And there are hundreds, even thousands of legal opinions out there that are relevant to teachers and other school personnel in some way. That's because the actions of school employees are, in many instances, attributable to the larger school system. Schools can be held legally liable for the actions of their employees. And in some cases, individual officials or school staff can be held legally liable for their own actions.

Many important legal opinions do get analyzed by your school or district and reflected in some way in those annual legal compliance meetings you've attended (or agonized through). But others don't. And it isn't always made clear that a lot of the dos and don'ts educators are told about in these meetings have their origin in a judicial opinion. By the time it reaches you, chances are the story and the rich history of a particular opinion have been stripped away, leaving you with just the grist, the bottom line.

A full accounting of all the relevant opinions published by judges on a daily basis in various jurisdictions is not possible within a short amount of time or the space allotted in this book. If you're like most busy educators, culling through centuries of jurisprudence is neither appealing nor the best use of your limited time, anyway.

So, for this book, I've selected just ten U.S. Supreme Court opinions involving public schools. Why these ten cases? Because they delve into some of the most important topics and situations educators face every day, including those at the beginning of this preface. They cover the landscape of both civil rights (discrimination) and civil liberties (individual freedom and privacy). Because they are U.S. Supreme Court cases, they impact the entire nation, not just one state or region. These are cases of historic impact that many people, not only educators, would benefit from knowing. And they're just plain interesting: They involve real problems of real people who are raising legal and policy issues thorny and weighty enough to have reached the highest court in the land. To read them is to take a mini-course in the history of education in our nation.

Most fundamentally, these cases serve as a reference and compass for educators, whose role as moral and civic leaders is more important than ever as our democracy becomes increasingly divisive and our futures uncertain. Other than the parent, it is *you*, the educator, who have long been the first responder when it comes to guiding children in how to treat others and engage with the world. You may be the first one to teach a child how to speak and even disagree with others respectfully, how to be kind, how to treat someone different as an equal. How important are those skills these days?

You, the educator, are a *legal* role model for kids—whether you see yourselves as such or not. Students watch how you interact not only with them but with other students and adults at school. They pick up on what behavior is permissible and what's out of bounds through you. That's what the law is, in essence: a system for mapping out and enforcing the norms of human behavior.

Beyond you, the classroom and entire school are a hotbed of civic (and arguably *legal*) learning, both passive and active. Students observe whether and how the rules and policies of the classroom and school are implemented. They notice how students with different backgrounds and abilities are treated. Students of color. Students from other nations. Students learning English. Students with cognitive or physical disabilities. Their civic and rudimentary "legal" education is constant, and yet—as opposed to subjects like math or language arts or science—there are few instructional resources on what the foundational principles or learning outcomes are in this type of education.

The foregoing cases illuminate these principles and outcomes for the educator. You may read them purely for your personal edification, but chances are you'll also be drawn to reflect on what they mean for your teaching practice or your school. How can they help you address the needs of a particular student? What civic lessons do they teach? What values do they impart?

You may be surprised to find that you are uncomfortable with how a particular case was decided; I personally disagree with the outcome of more than one in this bunch. But these cases still shed light on an important aspect of public education in the United States. Sometimes, seeing what we oppose can bring into focus what we espouse.

Reading these ten cases certainly won't address every situation educators encounter. Nor does it count as legal advice. But it will provide insights into how educators may act appropriately, support students who are at risk or face unique challenges or needs, and perhaps even elevate the discussion, teaching, and practice of equity and justice at school.

For each case, I provide a summary of the judicial opinion; some interesting history or perspective about someone involved in the case; a brief discussion of issues and legal concepts the case raises for educators; a sense of how the case impacts schools today, including more recent legal developments; tips or tales from educators and other people in the classroom or the community; and a short list of resources to further your knowledge about the case or the topics covered in it.

A quick word about advice or suggestions offered in this book: It's important to recognize that what may be required by a particular case (or by the law in general) is not the upper limit of what educators can or should do to address a particular situation. Most educators know intuitively that just because they aren't *legally* bound to act proactively or optimally to foster equity or non-discrimination doesn't mean they have no *professional, ethical, or personal* responsibility to do so. Accordingly, while many of the tips or suggestions in this book are not legally required by the Supreme Court cases they follow, they do reflect the kinds of behavior or practice that, in light of these cases, are designed to point educators in the right direction not only legally but professionally.

In conclusion, while there are certainly more than ten judicial opinions relevant to teaching, I hope you'll soon agree that these are ten exemplary cases to have gotten to know a little better. Perhaps reading about them will pique your interest in exploring them further—or in reading about other cases that have shaped the field of education and many of the values important to the functioning of our democracy.

CASE 1

Davis v. Monroe County Board of Education (1999)

Schools are responsible for appropriately addressing sexual harassment and violence among students.

oday, we might assume that schools are legally responsible for protecting students from harming each other. That responsibility seems like a logical outgrowth of the doctrine *in loco parentis*, in which schools assume the role of supervising kids in the stead of their parents or guardians.

But until fairly recently, there wasn't agreement on this. The conventional thinking was, sure, if a school *employee* harassed a student named Billy or Brenda—or if a school ignored a student's bullying of Billy while addressing similar bullying of Brenda—the school could be in legal hot water; but if Billy harassed Belinda (or vice versa) and the school didn't stop it, that was just a disciplinary issue within the school's discretion or, at most, a legal issue involving negligence or another personal injury.

The *Davis* case changed the landscape, making student-on-student aggression not just a legal issue but in many cases a civil rights issue.

LaShonda Davis attended the fifth grade at Hubbard Elementary School, a public school in Monroe County, Georgia. According to the legal complaint filed by her mother, in December 1992, a classmate, "G.F.," attempted to touch LaShonda's breasts and genital area and made vulgar statements such as "I want to get in bed with you" and "I want to feel your boobs." Similar conduct allegedly occurred in January of 1993.

In early February, G.F. purportedly placed a door stop in his pants and proceeded to act in a sexually suggestive manner toward LaShonda during physical education class. Approximately one week later, he again allegedly engaged in harassing behavior. The harassment occurred again in March, and again in April.

LaShonda's previously high grades allegedly dropped as she became unable to concentrate on her studies. In April, her father discovered that she had written a suicide note.

Finally, in May, G.F. was charged with, and pleaded guilty to, criminal sexual misconduct.

LaShonda's mother alleged that, after each of the harassing incidents, she or her daughter, and sometimes both of them, reported incidents to several different teachers at the school, but that no disciplinary action was taken in response.

LaShonda's mother also spoke with the school principal, who responded by stating he would have to "threaten" the harassing student "a little harder" and by asking why LaShonda "was the only one complaining."

And yet other girls also allegedly fell prey to G.F.'s conduct. At one point, a group composed of LaShonda and other female students tried to speak with the principal about G.F.'s behavior. But a teacher denied the students' request, saying, "If [the principal] wants you, he'll call you."

According to LaShonda's mother, no effort was made to separate G.F. and LaShonda, nor did the school board instruct its personnel on how to respond to peer sexual harassment or establish a policy on the issue.

THE CASE

In May 1994, LaShonda's mother filed suit on behalf of her daughter in federal court against the school board, the school district's superintendent, and the school principal. The complaint alleged that the "persistent sexual advances and harassment by the student G.F. upon [LaShonda] interfered with her ability to attend school and perform her studies and activities," and that "[t]he deliberate indifference by Defendants to the unwelcome sexual advances of a student upon LaShonda created an intimidating, hostile, offensive and abus[ive] school environment in violation of Title IX."

The federal law known as Title IX states: "[n]o person in the United States shall, on the basis of sex, be excluded from participation in, be denied the benefits of, or be subjected to discrimination under any education program or activity receiving Federal financial assistance."

The case made its way to the U.S. Supreme Court, which, on May 24, 1999, in an opinion written by Justice Sandra Day O'Connor, ruled in LaShonda Davis' favor, holding that the school district had violated her rights under Title IX.

THE DECISION

The Court affirmed that schools that receive federal funds (these can include private schools) are liable in money damages under Title IX only where they are *deliberately indifferent* to sexual harassment, of which they have *actual knowledge*, that is so *severe, pervasive, and objectively offensive* that it can be said to deprive the victims of access to the educational opportunities or benefits provided by the school.

This case established a nationwide precedent that a school that receives federal funding can violate Title IX by failing to respond appropriately to certain instances of harassment of a student not only by a school employee but also by another student (i.e., student-on-student harassment).

Verna Williams (at microphone), attorney for LaShonda Davis, speaks to reporters after her oral argument before the U.S. Supreme Court, as LaShonda's parents look on.

Today, Verna Williams is a respected dean and law professor at the University of Cincinnati College of Law. Two decades ago, however, she was a relatively junior attorney who, at the time she represented LaShonda Davis, had never argued in front of a court before. *Ever.* And yet she was the one LaShonda's parents chose to make her daughter's case before the U.S. Supreme Court, after another attorney withdrew from the case.

"The facts alleged in the complaint hit me hard," said Williams. "I had been ten once; I remembered the pain of being teased, but nothing, nothing like this." The victory would represent Williams' greatest triumph as a litigator.

Important Concepts

Deliberate Indifference

When one student harrases another, a school is not liable for monetary damages under Title IX unless it shows *deliberate indifference* to that harassment. This means a response or action by the school or school official that is clearly unreasonable in light of the known circumstances. The term also suggests that the school in some way had the ability to address the harm that befell the student victim; therefore, the harassment must have taken place in a context subject to the school district's control. To be liable for harassment under Title IX, the school must exercise substantial control over both the harasser and the context in which the known harassment occurs.

Actual Knowledge

This means that in order to be liable for harassment under Title IX, the school must be on notice that harassment has occurred. In other words, a school can't be held responsible for something it didn't know about or have any reason to know about. When a student or parent reports—verbally or in writing—an act of harassment to a teacher or principal, then the school is on notice. Also, when harassment occurs in plain sight, is widespread, or is well-known to students and staff, the school is very likely on notice. There are fuzzier situations, though. It often comes down to who said what, and to whom? Who saw what? It is safe to assume that when *almost any* school employee knows or has reason to know that harassment exists, the entire school is on notice.

Severe, Pervasive, and Objectively Offensive

In the context of student-on-student harassment, schools violate Title IX only when the student harasser's behavior is so *severe, pervasive, and objectively offensive* that it denies its victims equal access to education. Think of behavior that so undermines and detracts from the victim-students' educational experience that they are effectively denied equal access to an institution's resources and opportunities. Such behavior most likely does not include simple or isolated acts of teasing and name-calling among school children—hurtful or damaging as those acts may be. Whether gender-oriented conduct rises to the level of actionable harassment depends on a "constellation of surrounding circumstances, expectations, and relationships," including the ages of the harasser and the victim and the number of individuals involved. And one more piece of guidance (perhaps the most unnecessary line ever uttered by the U.S. Supreme Court): "Children may regularly interact in a manner that would be unacceptable among adults."

IMPLICATIONS FOR EDUCATORS AND SCHOOLS

- Teachers and school personnel should know who their designated Title IX coordinator is and find out to whom they are required to report acts of sexual harassment or violence. They should also know the basics of how to respond to incidents of harassment and what school resources are available for victims, perpetrators, or witnesses.

- Administrators should ensure that harassment and nondiscrimination policies and procedures are up-to-date and both communicated and visible to the school community and that personnel are appropriately trained on how to comply with federal, state, and local laws related to bullying, harassment, and violence. And they should ensure that they respond to harassment-related incidents appropriately and in a timely manner.

- "Bullying," "harassment," "sexual assault," "sexual violence": These terms connote different things to different people, but legally they often overlap. Instead of getting caught up in labels for offensive behavior, schools should evaluate the behavior itself—and whether it meets the criteria under the applicable laws to trigger legal liability on the part of the school or school personnel. Of course, even if a situation doesn't rise to the level of a legal problem, an appropriate response—educational, supportive, disciplinary, or policy-related—may still be warranted.

- Title IX (which prohibits sex discrimination) isn't the only federal law that addresses harassment. And federal law isn't the only game in town. School district policies likely cover this terrain as well and are the first place to look for guidance. Also, state laws (and state constitutions) are sometimes more specific and offer broader protections than federal laws.

Reflection

Take a moment to assess moments in your career as an educator when you witnessed acts of bullying, harassment, or social aggression among students or adults. Did you intervene? If so, how effective were you in preventing future acts? If not, why? What barriers did you face, and how might those barriers be removed?

GETTING PROACTIVE

Most educators know they should intervene when they witness bullying, harassment, or violence. That can mean directly stopping what's happening or finding an appropriate person to help stop what's happening if it's not safe for you to be physically involved directly. But educators can do much more to foster a safe and respectful school climate. Here are some proactive steps you can take:

- Watch your students for signs of injury, anxiety, or distress. Talk to them about it privately—or talk to a school counselor, administrator, or trusted colleague first—and come up with a plan.

- Review your district policies on bullying and harassment. (Seriously.) If you have questions, ask. Don't assume these policies are sacrosanct or comprehensive, but they are a good starting point.

- Start or join a faculty or student organization designed to foster safety, respect and equity—or lead an activity or curriculum in your classroom with similar goals.

Classroom AND Community VOICES

Tricia Ebarvia
High School English Teacher, Pennsylvania

As teachers, we wield tremendous power in classrooms, and that includes the power to establish a classroom environment that communicates mutual respect for all learners regardless of their gender. Because sexist and homophobic messages are pervasive in society, the most effective way to prevent issues of sexual harassment is to build anti-sexist, anti-homophobic norms in the classroom.

What makes this so difficult is that sexism—and sexual harassment—persists because of the many small ways in which we perpetuate it, even unintentionally. For example, using the term "guys" might seem like a gender-neutral term, but it reinforces male-dominant terms as "universal," while terms like "girls" or "gals" are clearly not. In a lesson on word choice, older students might discuss *The Atlantic* article, "The Problem with 'Hey Guys,'" by Joe Pinsker (Aug. 23, 2018, see at http://www.theatlantic.com).

We can help students use inclusive language by modeling this language ourselves. One small but potentially powerful change we can make as teachers to disrupt sexist language includes using gender-inclusive language when addressing the class; instead of "ladies and gentlemen" or "boys and girls," address the class as "scholars," "students," "friends," or "writers."

In addition, elementary students can be taught lessons about physical boundaries and appropriate and inappropriate touching. With older students, conversations about gender and equity can be integrated into existing lessons, particularly in the language arts. Issues of gender and sexism abound in many of the novels in many schools' curricula.

Rather than allowing potentially problematic gender stereotypes to go unchallenged in literature, invite students to think about how these stereotypes not only *reveal* sexist attitudes but also *contribute to sexism*—both when the text was written *and* today.

Additionally, because sexism and sexual harassment are rooted in power, as teachers we need to pay careful attention to the messages that we might send to students in our words and actions. In what ways do our unexamined biases perpetuate sexism in our classroom?

- Ask a colleague to observe and track your pattern of calling on students by using a simple tally based on gender. Take note both of the number of times some students speak as well as the number of minutes students hold the floor during conversation. What do you notice?

- Consider problematic statements such as "boys will be boys," especially when used as an excuse for behavior that can be inappropriate. When we excuse some behavior or hold different standards based on gender stereotypes, what messages do our students learn?

- Keep in mind that because gender is fluid, sexual harassment between students can manifest itself in many different ways as even students from the same self-identified gender group can harass or bully others.

Kara Pranikoff
Second-Grade Teacher, New York

If you ask my students what is most important to me as a teacher they will undoubtedly say safety first and, as a close second, that they are kind. While I care a great deal about academics and run a second-grade classroom that aims to challenge all learners, I never lose sight of the fact that I am raising human beings. Nothing is more important than their personhood, and we spend a good deal of time discussing, preparing for, and problem solving how to be good to our community in and out of the classroom.

Second grade is a complex and layered social year. Developmentally children begin to look outside of themselves and consider the thoughts and actions of others. They start to shift from their egocentric young selves to an awareness of the social realm. What other children say and think about them begins to matter. With this shift comes the responsibility on the teacher's end to nurture students who are able to listen openly, react respectfully, and give them the tools and practice they need to navigate their evolving social world with success. Here are three helpful tools that can support your young humans:

1. **Role play.** Take time to address the recurring challenges that happen in your classroom. Lead your students in role-playing activities, acting out common, often unproductive responses, and brainstorm, as a class, more respectful responses. Common situations you might address are: How to respond when someone hurts your feelings, when someone tells you that you cannot play with them, and when someone is not following a classroom or school rule.

2. **Develop upstanders.** We all know that challenging situations often occur out of earshot of the teacher—during recess, in the lunchroom, while walking in the halls. This is all the more reason that it's not enough to develop individual voices but to explain to your students the role of the "upstander." Books like *The Invisible Boy* by Trudy Ludwig and *I Walk with Vanessa* by Kerascoët provide clear examples of how to protect and stand up for a peer. Students need to speak up about what is good and true, regardless of what adult is listening.

3. **Recognize positive actions.** Communities are strong when it is their regular habit to function in care. Positive actions need to be recognized, not just by the adults but more importantly by their peers. Consider a method for your students to acknowledge the daily actions that support their community. Create a badge that they share with a peer when they make a move that helps the community—helping a friend, being flexible, making a compromise. This creates an atmosphere of recognition and gratitude that happens peer-to-peer, strengthening interactions from the ground up.

RECENT DEVELOPMENTS

In recent years, the federal government has actively enforced Title IX in its investigations of peer harassment of students who are gender-nonconforming. While Title IX does not specifically prohibit discrimination based on sexual orientation, it does prohibit sex discrimination of students who do not conform to gender stereotypes.

Students who are subjected to homophobic epithets or ridicule and other gender-based conduct that stem from commonly held perceptions about masculinity or femininity may be protected by Title IX.

The ubiquity of the Internet and smartphones means that harassment and bullying among students often take place in cyberspace—sometimes on school property, and sometimes at home. Whereas off-campus behavior unconnected to school activities has not traditionally been considered within a school's purview, in our increasingly interconnected world, courts and legislatures are recognizing at least some level of responsibility on the part of school officials over off-campus cyber-bullying or threatening behavior if that behavior has a real and palpable impact on the day-to-day activities of the school community. In other words, cyber-bullying—whether sexual in nature or not—is not only potentially devastating to those targeted but may also require schools to take actions to stop it, even if the texting, blogging, or posting occurs in locations outside traditional school boundaries.

GETTING MORE INFORMATION

Here's a list of mostly national-level organizations that can provide more in-depth information on bullying, harassment, and sexual violence. This list is not exhaustive. You may also wish to look up state and local resources, including resources offered by your own school district.

- American Psychological Association (see "Bullying"): http://www.apa.org/index.aspx

- Anti-Defamation League (see "Promoting Respectful Schools and Communities"): https://www.adl.org

- Equal Employment Opportunity Commission (see "Harassment"): https://www.eeoc.gov

- Gay, Lesbian & Straight Education Network (see "Educator Resources"): https://www.glsen.org

- Groundspark (see "Let's Get Real"): http://groundspark.org /our-films-and-campaigns/lets-get-real

- National Center on Safe Supportive Learning Environments: https://safesupportivelearning.ed.gov

- National Transgender Law Center (see "Know Your Rights in Schools"): http://www.transequality.org

- National Women's Law Center (see "Sexual Harassment and Assault"): https://nwlc.org

- Professional associations (see "Bullying and Harassment"): http://www.aft.org, http://www.aasa.org, https://www.naesp .org, https://www.nassp.org, http://www.nea.org, https:// www.nsba.org

- Stopbullying.gov: https://www.stopbullying.gov

- Teaching Tolerance (see "Professional Development: School Climate"): http://www.tolerance.org

- U.S. Department of Education Office for Civil Rights (see "Harassment Prevention Resources"): https://www2.ed.gov /about/offices/list/ocr/index.html

CASE 2.

Plyler v. Doe (1982)

Schools may not deny school-age children who are undocumented immigrants a free public education.

*H*ostility toward immigrants is nothing new; over two centuries, we've seen waves of public sentiment and even laws against immigrants who were Irish, German, Chinese, Japanese, Jewish, Muslim, and Mexican, to name just a few targeted groups. Today, much of the fervor surrounds immigrants from Latin America, with the building of a "wall" and the forced separations of migrant families at the U.S.–Mexico border dominating public discourse. The current anti-immigrant rhetoric and policies invite comparisons to a similar episode, occurring more than four decades ago, involving Mexican American students living in Texas.

When Alfredo Lopez was ten years old, he and his siblings were sent home from school and told they couldn't come back.

In 1977, Alfredo's school in Tyler, Texas, had adopted a policy to expel students who didn't have U.S. birth certificates. "All of a sudden, they could not go, because they were undocumented," said Alfredo's mother, Lídia Lopez.

Two years earlier Lídia Lopez had crossed the U.S.–Mexico border. She and her husband José found jobs picking roses. They were poor; their children sometimes helped in the rose fields while also attending school. It's no wonder that when the Tyler school district said the children could return to class if the family paid $1,000 per child, the Lopezes couldn't afford it.

Fortunately, the Lopezes came into contact with a social worker and eventually a lawyer who were willing to help them fight the school exclusion policy in court. "You have to have extraordinary will to actually want to go in there and take on the system and expose yourself to everything you're exposed to in litigation, and of course in this situation on top of that, this worry about being deported," their attorney, Larry Daves, explained.

The Lopezes *were* worried. In fact, on the morning of their hearing, they arrived at court with their most valuable belongings in case they had to escape being apprehended by immigration agents.

THE CASE

James Plyler was the superintendent of the Tyler Independent School District in Texas. The school district argued it had no choice but to charge tuition for undocumented students after the state of Texas passed a law in 1975 withholding any state funds for schools for the education of students who were not "legally admitted" to the United States. The Texas law also authorized local school districts to deny enrollment to children not "legally admitted" to the country.

"Doe" was one of several unnamed children of Mexican origin who could not prove through documentation that they were U.S. citizens or lawfully admitted to the United States. The students sued in federal court, arguing their rights to equal protection had been violated. The Fourteenth Amendment [to the U.S. Constitution] provides that "[n]o State shall . . . deprive any person of life, liberty, or property, without due process of law; nor deny to *any person within its jurisdiction* the equal protection of the laws."

The Tyler school district and the state of Texas argued that undocumented students, because of their immigration status, are not "persons within the jurisdiction" of the State of Texas, and that they therefore have no right to attend public schools on an equal basis as other students.

The case made its way to the U.S. Supreme Court. By a vote of 5 to 4, the Court rejected the argument of the state and the school district. Justice Brennan, writing for the majority, affirmed that undocumented immigrants are protected by the Fourteenth Amendment and that children who are undocumented must be allowed to attend public school on an equal basis as other children.

MAKING HISTORY

José and Lídia Lopez, parents of Alfredo Lopez

Alfredo Lopez graduated from high school in Tyler, Texas, and later worked as a truck driver and became a U.S. citizen. "My parents and the other three families [involved in the *Plyler* case], what they did, I guess, ended up being pretty important," he said. "For that we are thankful."

THE DECISION

The Court struck down a Texas law that refused to provide funds for undocumented children enrolled in local schools, as well as the local practice of charging tuition for undocumented students. (The Tyler school district had told parents that they had to pay $1,000 per undocumented child.) In doing so, the Court affirmed that the Fourteenth Amendment to the Constitution is not limited to the protection of citizens: "[T]he protection of the Fourteenth Amendment extends to anyone, citizen or stranger, who is subject to the laws of a State, and reaches into every corner of a State's territory." Unlawful entry into the United States did not impact this protection: "And until he leaves the jurisdiction—either voluntarily, or involuntarily in accordance with the Constitution and laws of the United States—he is entitled to the *equal protection* of the laws that a State may choose to establish" (emphasis added).

The Court also searched for a *rational basis* for the government's decision to deny immigrant children a public education. It failed to find one, noting the existence of a substantial "shadow population" and "underclass" of "illegal migrants" in the United States whose education was critical to maintain order and productivity in our society. "We cannot ignore the significant social costs borne by our Nation when select groups are denied the means to absorb the values and skills upon which our social order rests," it stated. "By denying these children a basic education, we deny them the ability to live within the structure of our civic institutions, and foreclose any realistic possibility that they will contribute in even the smallest way to the progress of our Nation."

(Clearly, while granting them a huge civil rights victory, the Court didn't go out of its way to extol the virtues or value of immigrants here, treating them instead like a pitiable caste whose influence on society needed to be managed, if not contained.)

The Court also specifically distinguished "innocent" children from their adult parents in the immigration context. It stated that, even if Texas found it useful to deter adults from illegal entry into the United States by refusing to provide a free education to their children, passing a law specifically to achieve that goal was fundamentally unjust to those children.

Significantly, the Court emphasized the importance of public education to democracy—a useful reminder given the uncertain support for public schools today:

> *We have recognized the public schools as a most vital civic institution for the preservation of a democratic system of government, and as the primary vehicle for transmitting the values on which our society rests . . . [E]ducation provides the basic tools by which individuals might lead economically productive lives . . . In sum, education has a fundamental role in maintaining the fabric of our society.*

Advocates for public schools and disadvantaged students savor this passage. It is one of the few times when the most powerful court in the land gave a full-throated defense of public education as a civic necessity.

Important Concept
Equal Protection

The Equal Protection Clause of the Fourteenth Amendment states that "no State shall . . . deny to any person within its jurisdiction the equal protection of the laws." These are perhaps the most powerful sixteen words in the history of modern civilization—and a great engine for civil rights, not only in the United States but worldwide, as other countries have modeled their constitutions after ours.

What does the Equal Protection Clause mean? Put simply: The government—including public schools—has to treat people who are similarly situated but for a single characteristic or trait (such as their race or their immigration status) equally.

To argue an "equal protection" violation, the plaintiff must show that she falls within a discrete class of people—Group A, if you will—who are being treated differently by the government than other people outside of that class—let's call them Group B. The equal protection challenge in *Plyler* involved comparing the treatment of school-age undocumented children of Mexican origin ("Group A") with the treatment of other children who were also attending Texas public schools ("Group B").

Rational Basis

Typically, in an equal protection case, the government must have a "rational basis" for treating a classification of people differently than others. Just as it sounds, "rationality" is not a very high bar: People do lots and lots of ill-advised, suboptimal, or just plain silly things that are not *irrational*.

When I teach the concept of equal protection to students, they are usually surprised to learn that there is a hierarchy in terms of the level of protection the law affords individuals in the United States depending on what kind of discrimination is being alleged. Some legal cases involving race or gender discrimination, or a small list of recognized fundamental rights, require the government to show more than just a rational basis for its actions; it must show that its actions were precisely tailored to serve a really important or even compelling interest of the government. *Plyler* was not one of those cases. In fact, the Court in *Plyler* bypassed the students' (plaintiffs') argument that they were victims of racial discrimination. The school district and the state of Texas (defendants) merely had to show some legitimate government interest (that is, a "rational basis"), rather than much stronger rationale, for treating students differently based on their immigration status. That's because, in our country, immigration status is lower in the legal chain of hierarchy than race or gender. It turns out that not all equal protection cases are equal.

The state of Texas made several justifications for its law barring education funds for undocumented children. This was its "rational basis" argument. The Court knocked every one of these down.

Preservation of the state's limited resources for the education of its lawful residents

"Of course, a concern for the preservation of resources standing alone can hardly justify the classification used in allocating those resources. The State must do more than justify its classification with a concise expression of an intention to discriminate."

Translation: Nice try, Texas, but you are basically saying you want to treat people unequally.

Protection from an influx of illegal immigrants

"There is no evidence in the record suggesting that illegal entrants impose any significant burden on the State's economy. To the contrary, the available evidence suggests that illegal aliens under-utilize public services, while contributing their labor to the local economy and tax money to the state fisc."

Translation: Your attempt to incite a panic over immigrants is not going to work.

Preserving high-quality education

"[T]he record in no way supports the claim that exclusion of undocumented children is likely to improve the overall quality of education in the State. In terms of educational cost and need . . . undocumented children are basically indistinguishable from legally resident alien children."

Translation: You haven't proved that kicking out the students who are undocumented will magically make schools better.

After dismissing these "rational basis" arguments, the Court described the *irrationality* of the government's actions, which "imposed a lifetime hardship" on undocumented students and "promot[ed] the creation and perpetuation of a subclass of illiterates within our boundaries, surely adding to the problems and costs of unemployment, welfare, and crime."

IMPLICATIONS FOR EDUCATORS AND SCHOOLS

- The most basic lesson for public schools is that they *must* matriculate otherwise eligible students regardless of their immigration status. Period.

- Beyond this, schools must not take actions during the enrollment process that may be difficult or intimidating for undocumented students or their families. For example, schools should not inquire about the immigration status of any student or family member.

- Schools may not *require* that students or their family members produce a birth certificate, proof of citizenship or lawful entry into the United States, or a Social Security card. Schools may legitimately ask for proof of age, or proof of residency within the school district boundary (except for homeless students)—but families should be able to verify this information in a variety of ways.

- Many families become separated because of the detention or deportation of a parent or guardian. Schools should be prepared to matriculate unaccompanied minors—including those who are released from federal custody to an appropriate sponsor, usually a family member.

- Immigration-related enforcement actions (including "raids") are not to occur at or be focused on sensitive locations such as public school unless (1) "exigent circumstances" exist, (2) other law enforcement actions have led officers to the school, or

(3) prior approval is obtained from a designated school official. Even so, immigration enforcement around the nation has significantly impacted schools, including massive attendance drop-offs and increased student anxiety and health problems.

- Privacy laws prohibit schools from providing, without parental consent, student-related information to federal immigration agents if the information would potentially expose a student's immigration status. Even if federal immigration agents present a school with a deportation order or warrant, the school is still permitted to refrain from providing student information, as the warrant is administrative, not judicial.

- Educators play an enormously important role in helping all students to understand the lives of and reduce hostility toward immigrants, including undocumented immigrants. Educators can do much by helping students to feel safe at school and by recognizing the signs of stress or anxiety in students because of immigration policies or enforcement.

Reflection

What challenges do undocumented children (or children of undocumented parents or guardians) face at your school? Do any other students face similar challenges (for example, a homeless student or a student coping with the loss or incarceration of a family member)? How do these challenges affect you as an educator? What is your role to help these students?

GETTING PROACTIVE

- Help your school system adopt clear principles, policies, and practices related to immigration-related situations, including how it will handle contacts with immigration enforcement and support students and families who may be impacted by immigration.

- Facilitate educator training on immigration-related laws, students' rights, and schools' obligations.

- In the classroom, explore myths and stereotypes involving immigrants with your students, and work together to dispel them.

- Create a safe learning environment for immigrant students. Don't reveal the status of undocumented students or ask them to self-identify. Use terms such as "undocumented immigrant" rather than "illegal" or "alien." Identify as an ally through your words and lessons and by displaying signs and symbols that your classroom is a safe space for immigrant students.

Classroom AND Community VOICES

Julie Jee
High School English Teacher, New York

When I think of the *Plyler* case, I think of what would lead elected officials or school administrators to want to shut out a whole class of immigrant children from our schools. I draw connections to what is going on today, with hostility toward immigrants, and Muslims in particular. I led a class study of *Love, Hate and Other Filters* by Samira Ahmed. My sophomores and I watched the TED Talk: *Islamophobia Killed My Brother* (https://www.youtube.com/watch?v=XiEQmcZi8cM). We talked about what happened to Suzanne Barakat's brother and friends and how Islamophobia is hurting the protagonist, Maya, and her family after a terrorist attack occurred and the suspect happened to have the same last name as them. Understanding others' stories is a big step in developing compassion and understanding. It also helps my students understand how inequality can develop and play out in the real world, such as in the *Plyler* case.

RECENT DEVELOPMENTS

Since the *Plyler* case, there have been other attempts to bar undocumented children from school. For example, in the 1990s in California, voters passed Proposition 187, which would have barred undocumented people from public services, including public education. The courts blocked the measure from taking effect.

The Trump administration has stepped up deportation enforcement actions against undocumented persons in the United States. Immigration raids around schools have significantly impacted schools themselves, with some schools experiencing dramatic attendance drops following raids of surrounding workplaces. In a recent UCLA survey, 84 percent of educators reported that students expressed worries about the effects of immigration enforcement, and more than 60 percent of educators observed a downturn in academic performance for students affected by immigration enforcement. Educators themselves have experienced additional stress and workload burden from immigration enforcement.

"One of my students let me know that she was going to court with her parents the next day," a high school teacher in New York told me. "There was a strong possibility that they were going to get deported, so she would have to leave the country with them. I was deeply affected by her situation. So many children have uncertain futures. These undocumented students and their family members are being affected emotionally and psychologically. The anxiety is real."

The Trump administration also announced in 2017 that it intended to end the Deferred Action for Childhood Arrivals (DACA) program—which protects eligible immigrant youth who came to the United States when they were children from deportation. (Because of litigation, however, DACA is still alive for prior DACA recipients as of the time of this publication.) DACA or no DACA, undocumented students still have a right to attend school, under *Plyler*.

Congress has also yet to pass what is known as The DREAM Act (short for Development, Relief and Education for Alien Minors Act), which would grant legal status to certain undocumented immigrants who were brought to the United States as minors. Because of this legislation, people who are undocumented and who have gone to school and lived in the United States are sometimes referred to as "Dreamers."

GETTING MORE INFORMATION

Here's a list of organizations that can provide more in-depth information on students, immigration, and the law. This list is not exhaustive. You may also wish to look up state and local resources, including resources offered by your own school district.

- American Federation of Teachers (see "Immigration"): www.aft.org

- Immigration Legal Resource Center (see "Immigration Resources for Teachers and Educators"): www.ilrc.org

- Immigrants Rising (see "Resources"): https://immigrants rising.org

- Library of Congress (see "Immigration Lesson Plans"): www.loc.gov

- Migration Policy Institute (see "K–12 Education"): www.migrationpolicy.org

- UCLA Civil Rights Project (see "Immigration Research"): www.civilrightsproject.ucla.edu

- U.S. Department of Education (see "Fact Sheet: Information on the Rights of All Children to Enroll in School"; and "Information on the Rights of Unaccompanied Children to Enroll in School and Participate Meaningfully and Equally in Educational Programs"): www.ed.gov

CASE 3

Parents Involved in Community Schools v. Seattle School District No. 1 (2007)

Schools can take steps to increase student racial diversity—but need to be careful in how they do it.

Most of us who didn't attend school during the civil rights era have at least studied *Brown v. Board of Education*—the landmark U.S. Supreme Court school desegregation case from 1954. Separate is not equal, the Court declared. And so, schools must racially integrate. The following year, Rosa Parks refused to move to the back of the bus. The Jim Crow era was dying. The civil rights movement had sprung to the fore.

Thanks to pro-desegregation governmental and judicial policies and enforcement, by the late 1980s the segregation of black and white students in the South had reached a low point. But by then, a growing backlash against and rollback of pro-desegregation policies and protections had begun to take its toll. Today, all of the desegregation gains in the South achieved since 1967 have been wiped out, and schools throughout the nation remain deeply segregated by race. And in recent decades, parents—several of them white—have filed lawsuits to contest school assignments that furthered racial diversity but, in their view, harmed their own children's education.

Kathleen Brose—a PTA member, volunteer music teacher, and mother of two—was one of those parents. In 1999, she followed the city of Seattle's application process to enroll her daughter Elisabeth in high school, hoping that Elisabeth would end up at her first choice: Ballard High, nestled on a thirteen-acre campus replete with state-of-the-arts facilities including a genetics lab, a tournament-class gymnasium, an 8,200-square-foot library, and a TV production studio. But Elisabeth ended up at her fourth choice, Franklin High, which her mother described as a "heavily black school with lower test scores."

Kathleen attributed this result to Seattle's brand-new school assignment system, which included a "tiebreaker" policy aimed at ensuring racial diversity in schools. She believed her daughter, who is white, had been discriminated against. And so, as president of a new organization called Parents Involved in Community Schools, she decided to fight this result in court.

THE CASE

Kathleen Brose was just one of several Seattle parents in the organization called Parents Involved in Community Schools who challenged the city's student-assignment system in court.

For example, another parent in Seattle sought to enroll her ninth-grade son, Andy, in Ballard High School. Andy suffered from attention deficit hyperactivity disorder and dyslexia but had made good progress with hands-on instruction, and Ballard's biotechnology program held the most promise for his continued success. Andy was accepted into this selective program but, because of the racial tiebreaker policy, was denied a spot there.

It's important to note that Seattle's student-assignment plan was not created in a vacuum: In fact, it followed decades of widespread racial segregation in schools, lawsuits brought by the NAACP, and a mandatory busing policy, which was abandoned in 1988 due in part to its unpopularity, cost, and negative effect on white enrollment in public schools.

In 1998, Seattle adopted a new plan for assigning students to its ten public high schools. The plan allowed incoming ninth-graders to choose from among any of the district's high schools, ranking however many schools they wish in order of preference. If too many students listed the same school as their first choice, the district employed a "tiebreaker" to admit students who had a sibling currently enrolled in the chosen school.

But the next tiebreaker in Seattle's school-assignment system depended upon the racial composition of the particular school and the race of the individual student. If an oversubscribed school was not within 10 percentage points of the district's overall white/nonwhite racial balance, the district used a tiebreaker to select students whose race would serve to bring the school into balance.

This was the system that did not assign Elisabeth and Andy to their first-choice schools.

Meanwhile, all the way across the country in Louisville, Kentucky, a similar situation was unfolding. Meredith, a parent in Jefferson County, sought to enroll her son Joshua in a kindergarten only a mile from his new home, but it had no available space. So, the district assigned Joshua to another elementary school in his assigned "cluster," Young Elementary School. That school was ten miles from home, and so Meredith sought to transfer Joshua to another school in a different cluster, which happened to be much closer to home. But the transfer was denied because it would have an adverse effect on the racial diversity of Young Elementary.

As in Washington State, there was a long history involving race and schooling in Kentucky. The Louisville school district within Jefferson County had been operating under a school desegregation consent decree since 1975. This meant that the district had been determined to be unlawfully segregated and had been placed under court supervision to desegregate. In this respect, it was no

MAKING HISTORY

Kathleen Brose, left, and her lawyers spoke to reporters after the Supreme Court ruling.

After learning that the Supreme Court had ruled in her favor, Kathleen Brose said, "I was relieved that we won. I felt vindicated that the seven years of work paid off. I'm glad for the city of Seattle and for the school district. Let's move beyond race and pay attention to the school districts and fix them." While her daughter Elisabeth had already graduated from high school, her younger daughter would attend Ballard High School—the school at which she had fought to get Elisabeth placed.

Brose maintains that she was against discrimination, not racial diversity. But in examining the trendlines, it's hard not to draw a correlation between the *Parents Involved* case and decreased racial diversity. Nearly six times as many schools in Seattle are classified as intensely segregated (meaning that 90 percent or more of the students in those schools are non-white) today, than was the case in 1990. Sean Riley, an African American who is both a product of and an educator in Seattle public schools, observes: "Racial balance is long gone in most Seattle schools. Schools that in my childhood were nearly half white and nonwhite are nearly all-minority again. Twenty of Seattle's schools consist of 90 percent or more students of color. Seattle isn't only resegregating; the district as a whole is becoming less diverse."

different from hundreds of other school districts around the nation in the decades immediately following *Brown v. Board of Education*. Decades of court-supervised actions, including multiple revisions of the student-assignment plan, ensued. Then, in 1999, a group of parents sued to stop the use of race to assign students to magnet schools within the district. A federal court judge agreed, deeming that practice unconstitutional and dissolving the desegregation order because, in the court's opinion, the school board had exercised "good faith compliance" with the order.

After the decree was dissolved in 2000, the Louisville district followed a voluntary desegregation plan in which all non-magnet public schools were to maintain a racial composition that was at least 15 percent but no more than 50 percent black. Students could pick a preference for a school within their assigned cluster, but if the student composition within their chosen school was at the extremes of the racial guidelines, a student whose race would contribute to racial imbalance would not be assigned to that school.

This was the system that denied Joshua his preferred choice of school. His mother sued on his behalf.

The Kentucky case was eventually combined with the Seattle case to form what would become the *Parents Involved* case before the U.S. Supreme Court.

On June 28, 2007, in a 5 to 4 vote, Chief Justice Roberts held that the two school districts' student assignment plans violated the Equal Protection Clause of the Fourteenth Amendment of the U.S. Constitution and that the racial classifications employed by the districts were not "narrowly tailored to the goal of achieving . . . racial diversity" but rather "directed only to racial balance, pure and simple, an objective this Court has repeatedly condemned as illegitimate."

THE DECISION

In striking down the Seattle and Jefferson County student-assignment plans, the Court appeared troubled by the fact that race figured so prominently in how students in these districts were assigned to particular schools. This, according to the Court, was in contrast to prior affirmative action cases in the higher education context, in which an individual student's race was but one factor among many in the admissions process.

The Court didn't like the way in which the districts defined racial diversity in binary fashion—viewing race exclusively as "white/ nonwhite" or "black/ other"—which seemingly discounted the presence of Asian American, Native American, or Latinx students.

The Court also said that the student-assignment plans required the district to "work backward" to achieve a "racial balance" that was mechanically tied to racial demographics within the district, rather than "work forward" to produce a level of diversity needed to create some purported educational benefit.

In the end, the Court boiled down the districts' integration efforts to a system of "racial balancing," thus dooming them. If any principle emerges from this ruling, it is that the

IN FACT

Public schools became more racially integrated in the thirty years after *Brown v. Board.* In the next thirty years, however, after a series of U.S. Supreme Court rulings weakened court protection and oversight over desegregation, racial isolation in schools has increased. During the quarter century since 1988— the high point of desegregation in the U.S.—the share of public schools whose student racial composition is 90 percent non-white or greater has more than tripled, rising from 5.7 percent to 18.6 percent of all public schools.

Fast-forward sixty-five years. Today, nearly one out of five public schools in the United States is highly segregated. Fewer and fewer school districts are under court supervision to desegregate. Schools exist in neighborhoods and regions increasingly divided by race and class, with few mandates or incentives for schools to matriculate students from areas outside of established school attendance zones. Indeed, there has been for some time the sense that schools *cannot* take extraordinary steps to diversify, with the era of inter-district busing long since past and a more rigid, "colorblind" approach prevailing in education policy circles.

government must treat people as individuals, not simply as "components" of a racial identity or group.

While it's hard to dispute that principle, I find it highly irritating, as a civil rights lawyer, to realize that the Court used the same legal doctrine used in *Brown v. Board of Education* to mandate desegregation (equal protection) in order to *invalidate* desegregation efforts in *Parents Involved*, without taking into account the extensive desegregation efforts the Seattle and Jefferson County districts made to comply with *Brown* in the first place.

What are we left with after this case? First and foremost, public schools that are not under some existing desegregation order must consider how to diversify racially without thinking about race first, using *race-neutral alternatives*. They have to show that such alternatives are unworkable before they can look into students' race specifically. But schools can also immediately pursue *general policies* that increase racial diversity, as long as those policies don't involve looking at students' individual race.

Important Concepts

Race-Neutral Alternatives

The Seattle and Jefferson County school districts had to show that they considered methods other than explicit racial classifications to achieve their stated goals. The Court said that they failed to do this, pointing to Seattle's rejection of several alternative assignment plans that did not involve racial classifications as well as Jefferson County's failure to present any evidence that it considered alternatives to racial classifications (for example, income-based classifications or a non-race-based lottery system for assigning students to schools).

General vs. Student-Specific Policies

One of the most critical points in *Parents Involved* was made by Justice Kennedy in a separate, concurring opinion (which means that it wasn't part of the majority opinion but can still be influential to schools and to future cases in this area):

If school authorities are concerned that the student-body compositions of certain schools interfere with the objective of offering equal educational opportunity to all of their students, they are free to devise race-conscious measures to address the problem in a general way and without treating each student in different fashion solely on the basis of a systemic, individual typing by race.

Justice Kennedy gave the following examples of how schools could diversify in a race-conscious manner without resorting to individual racial classification of students:

- Selecting new school sites strategically to improve racial composition of student body.
- Drawing attendance zones with the racial demographics of neighborhoods in mind.
- Allocating resources for special programs to attract a diverse student body.
- Recruiting students and faculty in a racially targeted fashion.
- Tracking enrollments, performance, and other statistics by race.

All of the above actions, if done in a way to invite or attract students of different races to particular schools, do not set hard racial quotas or classify and assign individual students according to their race and would presumably survive legal challenges. But *Parents Involved* may have scared school boards from even pursuing these perfectly legitimate strategies to foster racial integration.

IMPLICATIONS FOR EDUCATORS AND SCHOOLS

- For schools today, the options to influence racial diversity fall into three categories: use race-conscious measures and justify them in a way described by the Court in *Parents Involved*; use race-neutral alternatives; or do nothing. Which strategy your school district has pursued is largely up to your district board and its lawyers. Having said this, as key members of the school community, you may be interested in learning more about where your school stands on racial diversity and how racially diverse your school is relative to other schools in the district or the district at large. Find the racial composition and demographics of students at your school and in your district using the Civil Rights Data Collection: https://ocrdata.ed.gov.

- Learn more about notable school integration efforts in other cities such as Hartford, CT; Lower Merion, PA; Berkeley, CA; Cambridge, MA—and even Jefferson County, KY, in the aftermath of the *Parents Involved* case. (For starters, you might visit The Century Foundation website at https://tcf.org).

Reflection

We know from court desegregation orders from the civil rights era that the racial composition of schools is only one facet of the problem of unequal educational opportunity. The problem of segregative (discriminatory) behavior *within* schools and districts—providing fewer educational opportunities and challenging curricular options for, and more severely disciplining, students who are racial minorities—has also been prevalent. Data suggest that this problem remains in many schools today. How can educators grapple with disparities in treatment that exist *within* schools and districts? And do they have any role or responsibility in addressing disparities and racial segregation/isolation *between* schools and districts?

GETTING PROACTIVE

You have little or no control over the racial composition of your classroom, but that doesn't mean you can't learn more about how students get assigned to you—or how to address racial inequities in how education is delivered *within* schools or classrooms.

- Learn how your district or school selects its students and whether the race of students plays any role in student assignments; this information may be available online or through your district office.

- Look closely at your school's honors and AP class enrollment data. (You can find school-level data at https://ocrdata.ed.gov.) At the classroom level, develop strategies and build supports for students who are underrepresented in those classes.

Classroom AND Community VOICES

Kim Parker
High School English Teacher, Massachusetts

I taught English at a high school in Cambridge, Massachusetts, that tracks students. Most of the students in the lowest-level classes (called College Prep) were people of color, while most of the students in Honors and AP classes were white. I decided to detrack my sophomore class because I didn't want to be complicit in a system that denies opportunities to young people of color.

I piloted a year-long class called Honors Prep. My goal was to move my College Prep (CP) students into the Honors English track. I knew that if I could prepare them for success in advanced classes, their entire high school trajectory could change. We focused on developing reading skills, stamina, and fostering a love of literacy. These parallel skills were ones students could practice and master with their peers as they gained comfort asking questions, dispelling misunderstand-ings about what happens in Honors classes, and developing any lagging academic skills. At the end of the first semester of the Honors Prep pilot, my CP students moved into my Honors English class. Drawing on the work from the previous semester, I was able to build and deepen the work students did, spending more time on teaching complex texts, refining writing skills, and building students' self-confidence and resilience.

I taught Honors Prep for two years and was able to move nearly fifty young people into the Honors track. My students demonstrated, time and again, that they were able to complete challenging work if they were taught and given the time to be-come proficient in the necessary skills.

RECENT DEVELOPMENTS

- The school-age population is more diverse than ever—in 2014, for the first time, nationwide, more than 50 percent of the school-age population was non-white. And yet, as mentioned earlier, schools are resegregating at a fast rate. Today, for ex-ample, in the state of New York, nearly two out of three black and Latinx students attend schools that are overwhelmingly (90 percent or above) black and Latinx—and admission poli-cies to specialized New York City high schools that exacerbate segregation are a current flashpoint in local politics there.

- As mentioned earlier, in the *Parents Involved* case, Justice Kennedy articulated a strategy by which schools could pursue *general* (i.e., non-individual-specific) policies to diversify without considering every student's race before assigning them to a school. School districts have done just this and survived legal challenges. For example, within the past decade, Lower Merion School District in Pennsylvania adopted a redistricting plan that, in the view of a federal appeals court, "passed constitutional muster because it [did] not select students based on racial classifications, [did] not use race to assign benefits or burdens in the school assignment process, [did] not apply the plan in a discriminatory manner, and [did] not have a racially discriminatory purpose."

In 2018, the Trump administration rescinded a U.S. Department of Education policy on the "voluntary use of race" in student assignment. That Obama administration policy guidance, released in 2012, articulated the Department's interpretation of the *Parents Involved* case in a way that suggested that school districts could pursue race-conscious student-assignment strategies as long as they pursued race-neutral strategies first and/or general (not student-specific) diversity strategies (see "Important Concepts" earlier in this chapter). The rescission of the Obama-era guidance signals the Trump administration's narrower interpretation of *Parents Involved* and possibly its intent to investigate schools that take *any* measures to impact the racial composition of their schools—an ominous development for those wanting to achieve greater diversity in their schools.

GETTING MORE INFORMATION

Here's a list of organizations that can provide more in-depth information, research, and data on school diversity and school segregation in the United States:

- The Century Foundation: https://tcf.org/content/report/school-integration-practice-lessons-nine-districts/
- The National Archives: https://www.archives.gov/education/lessons/desegregation

- National Coalition on School Diversity: http://school-diversity.org

- The National Park Service: https://www.nps.gov/brvb/index.htm (see *Brown v. Board* National Historical Site)

- Poverty & Race Research Action Council (PRRAC): https://prrac.org

- Teaching Tolerance: https://www.tolerance.org/magazine/spring-2004/brown-v-board-timeline-of-school-integration-in-the-us (see *Brown v. Board*: Timeline of School Integration in the U.S.)

- UCLA Civil Rights Project: www.civilrightsproject.ucla.edu

- The Urban Institute: https://www.urban.org/research-area/racial-segregation

Endrew F. v. Douglas County School District (2017)

Students with disabilities are entitled to an education reasonably calculated to enable them to make progress.

Millions of educators are familiar with the IEP—that is, the Individualized Education Plan—that each child with a disability is entitled to in public school. The basic parameters of the IEP, and the entitlement of students with disabilities to a "free appropriate public education" (or FAPE), were established by the Supreme Court in 1982 in the *Rowley* case. But the Court never defined what level of education was enough to satisfy the law. Enter *Endrew F.*

Endrew F., who goes by "Drew," was diagnosed with autism at age two. He attended school in the Douglas County School District in Colorado from preschool through fourth grade. His teachers described him as a humorous kid with a sweet disposition who showed concern for his friends.

Each year, his IEP team drafted a plan to address his educational and functional needs. Things started going south as Drew's elementary school career progressed. For one thing, the school stopped allowing Drew's parents to use a private therapist, paid from their own money, to come to the school and consult with Drew's teachers.

By the fourth grade, Drew's parents had become dissatisfied with his progress. His IEP seemed to be repetitive, carrying over the same basic goals and objectives from one year to the next.

Then Jennifer, Drew's mom, began to receive calls from the school to come manage her son or take him home. To be sure, Drew had behavioral problems that inhibited his learning: He would scream in class, climb over furniture and other students, and even run away from school. He also had a fear of flies, spills, and public restrooms.

As documented in the Supreme Court case, the IEP process didn't address Drew's academic and behavioral problems. According to Joe, Drew's dad, Drew was being "babysat" at school.

In 2010, the school district presented Drew's parents with a fifth-grade IEP that was, in their view, pretty much the same as his past ones. So, his parents removed him from public school and enrolled him at a private school that specializes in educating children with autism.

The private school where Drew's parents enrolled him was a twenty-five-minute drive from their home. The tuition was $65,000 a year. But Drew reportedly thrived there; according to Joe, Drew was "a different kid" and "not afraid of everything at school."

The private school developed a behavioral intervention plan that identified Drew's most problematic behaviors and set out particular strategies for addressing them. It also added more rigor to his academic program. Within months, Drew's behavior improved significantly, as did his academic performance.

With this new evidence in hand, Drew's parents returned to his old public school to seek to chart a better course for their son. But the district presented a fifth-grade IEP that, in their view, was no better than the one it had proposed earlier—and not all that different from Drew's fourth-grade IEP.

MAKING HISTORY

Endrew F., a student with autism, secured an important U.S. Supreme Court victory for students with disabilities.

In 2018, a federal judge went on to rule that Drew's parents, Jennifer and Joe, were entitled to reimbursement for Drew's tuition and their legal costs. The school district settled the case with them. The parents received $1.3 million.

Drew's parents feel gratified by the larger implications of the Supreme Court decision. "It was an opportunity to hopefully make a difference for six-and-a-half-million kids on IEPs," said Jennifer. And Joe thinks the ruling "put schools on notice" that they can't "provide a child a meaningless education" regardless of their ability status.

As for Drew? His parents say he is a homebody who likes peanut butter and jelly sandwiches, cats, video games, and Pixar movies. He will stay happily enrolled at his private school until he turns 21.

In 2012, Jennifer and Joe filed a complaint with the Colorado Department of Education seeking reimbursement for Drew's tuition at the private school. They argued that the school district had not provided Drew an appropriate education in a timely manner, as required by law. Their request was denied.

Undeterred, they sued the district on behalf of their son in federal court.

THE CASE

The case made its way to the U.S. Supreme Court. By then, Drew was seventeen years old.

On March 22, 2017, in an opinion written by Chief Justice John Roberts, the Court unanimously held that "[w]hen all is said and done, a student offered an educational program providing 'merely more than [minimal]' progress from year to year can hardly be said to have been offered an education at all. The IDEA [Individuals with Disabilities Education Act] demands more. It requires an educational program reasonably calculated to enable a child to make progress appropriate in light of the child's circumstances."

THE DECISION

The Court rebuffed the school district's argument that a child's IEP is adequate as long as it is calculated to confer an educational benefit that enables him or her to make *some* progress that is more than merely *de minimis* (that's legalese for very small or trivial). Instead, the Court stated that a school must offer an IEP reasonably calculated to enable a child to make progress appropriate in light of the child's circumstances.

The overall legal obligation of schools remains the same: Schools must provide a free appropriate public education (FAPE) to children with disabilities that includes both "special education" and "related services." Special education is "specially designed instruction to meet the unique needs of a child with a disability." Related services are the support services "required to assist a child to benefit from" that instruction.

Important Concepts

The Court established that an IEP must be *reasonably calculated* for the child to make *progress appropriate . . . in light of the child's circumstances.*

So, what's "appropriate" progress? What's a "reasonable calculation" of that progress? And what about that qualifier, "in light of a child's circumstances"?

Appropriate Progress

The Court in *Endrew F.* explained that, while each child's situation is unique, for disabled children who are integrated into the regular classroom with other children, the IEP program should be fashioned to enable them to "achieve passing marks and advance from grade to grade." And for children with disabilities outside of the regular classroom, the educational program must be "appropriately ambitious" for their unique circumstances and give them the "chance to meet challenging objectives."

Reasonably Calculated

The Court stated that the school should engage in a "fact-intensive exercise" that is "informed not only by the expertise of school officials, but also by the input of the child's parents or guardians" in order to ensure the IEP is "reasonably calculated" for the child to make progress. The court also cautioned that "reasonable" does not necessarily mean "ideal." Here, the Court seems to be saying that there is a predictive or uncertain element to the IEP formation process that cannot always be completed with fine-tuned precision.

In Light of the Child's Circumstances

The Court made clear that, under the IDEA, every child is to be considered unique and that what's appropriate for each will differ from child to child. Schools need to assess each child's "present levels of achievement, disability, and potential for growth." Given the wide spectrum of children with disabilities, "the benefits obtainable by children at one end of the spectrum will differ dramatically from those obtainable by children at the other end, with infinite variations in between."

IN FACT

Thirteen percent (6.7 million) of all students in public schools receive special education services. Between 2009 and 2016, the U.S. Department of Education received 36,790 disability-related civil rights complaints from students and parents nationwide. Nearly half of the complaints related to allegations that schools failed to provide a free appropriate public education (FAPE), and nearly one in five complaints related to allegations of unfair treatment and denial of disability-related benefits. Other complaint areas involving students with disabilities related to the accessibility of educational technology and websites, accessibility of programs and facilities, and discrimination in admissions.

These terms may seem impossibly fuzzy—kind of like being thrown back into the wilderness of the unknown. But here's what we now know: IEPs that look very similar from year to year (like those designed for Drew) will have a tougher time passing legal muster than before. Sure, there could be a situation involving a particular child who can't progress that much from year to year relative to other children. But the Court is signaling that, even in that scenario, the child's IEP should reflect significant and meaningful progress appropriate *for that child.*

IMPLICATIONS FOR EDUCATORS AND SCHOOLS

- *Endrew F.* is a case that addresses the standard under the IDEA for ensuring that students with disabilities receive an education that is challenging and appropriate. Other disability-related antidiscrimination laws include Section 504 of the Rehabilitation Act of 1973 (Section 504) and the Americans with Disabilities Act (ADA). And there's also the federal school funding and accountability law, called the Every Student Succeeds Act, or ESSA (formerly known as the No Child Left Behind Act). ESSA also requires that students with disabilities grow or improve academically. In this regard, ESSA and the disability-specific laws operate loosely in tandem with one another.

- Early identification and evaluation (as early as preschool) of whether a student may have a disability is an important first step. Here's one resource that can help educators spot certain learning disabilities: http://www.ldonline.org/ldbasics/signs

- A student who has one of thirteen specific conditions (including physical, emotional, and learning disabilities and other health impairments) may qualify for special education and related services (and an IEP) under the IDEA. Other students may qualify as disabled under Section 504 or the ADA and be entitled to accommodations and related services, to be specified in a "504 Plan" in lieu of an IEP.

- In general, students covered under Section 504 or the ADA must (1) have a physical or mental impairment that substantially limits one or more major life activities (including not only walking, seeing, or hearing, but also learning); (2) have a record of such an impairment; or (3) be regarded as having such an impairment.

- Close communication with and involvement of parents and guardians prior to and during the evaluation and placement of students with disabilities is a good rule of thumb.

- Given that pretty much all public school employees—not just special education teachers—interact with students with disabilities or learning challenges, it's important that schools offer regular and effective professional development for all school staff on the educational and school climate needs of students with disabilities.

Reflection

Educators often grapple with the tension between ensuring individual and specialized attention for students with disabilities and educating such students in the most integrated and least restrictive environment possible. Another difficulty educators face is the need to accurately identify students for special education and related services while simultaneously avoiding the inaccurate classification of students (including students of color or English learners) as needing special education. How do you manage these tensions? What supports do you have to address them?

GETTING PROACTIVE

As educators who have taught and worked with students with disabilities, you know the importance of early diagnosis and intervention, thoughtful crafting of IEPs, and regular communication with parents and guardians. Here a few other ideas:

- The IDEA requires that students with disabilities be educated in the regular classroom environment to the extent possible. Evaluate whether there may be students who are being unnecessarily separated from nondisabled students.

- As you or your school utilize online or electronic learning platforms, curricula, testing, or communications with students and parents, be sure that they (and any associated devices or technology) are accessible and adaptable to persons with disabilities, including those who have visual or hearing impairments or limited mobility. For tips, school IT specialists can ensure that school websites comply with accessibility standards adopted by the World Wide Web Consortium (W3C) at https://www.w3.org.

- Data from around the nation shows that students with disabilities are disproportionately bullied, disciplined, and subjected to other potentially harmful conditions (including restraint and seclusion) compared with non-disabled students. Look up the statistics for your school at https://ocrdata.ed.gov, and discuss with colleagues whether changes in policy and practice may be warranted.

Classroom AND Community VOICES

Jamaica Ross
Elementary School Teacher, California

When I read about this case, it made me think of Thomas [name changed to protect his privacy], who was an eight-year-old in my third-grade classroom. Thomas was diagnosed with merosin-deficient congenital muscular dystrophy at age three. He is non-ambulatory. In addition to his physical needs, Thomas qualified for special education services due to his specific learning disability. He received reading, writing, and math support from the Resource Specialist Personnel (RSP), who agreed to work with him in my classroom as opposed to pulling him out.

The RSP teacher and I created a plan and made accommodations that addressed Thomas's IEP goals. In math, he was provided with the tools that best supported his learning style. He typically learned best when he could use manipulatives such as base ten blocks and counters. He preferred a number line and lists of skip-counting patterns to support all operations. In other content areas, he received direct vocabulary instruction and extended time to build knowledge in order to understand more abstract concepts. We unpacked word problems and applied learning in leveled small groups.

Physically, Thomas wanted to spend more time out of his wheelchair. He tested his boundaries and independence by trying different chairs and spaces. During learning time, he could choose his learning space, as my classroom had a flexible seating environment.

All of the structures in our class—morning circle, small-group instruction, flexible seating—are planned and intentional. I take steps to address the needs of all my students, especially those with additional needs. I work with all my students to find what works best for their learning and what kind of environment and teaching help them feel successful and comfortable.

RECENT DEVELOPMENTS

What's changed since *Endrew F.*? It may be too soon to tell. For what it's worth, school districts are still winning the vast majority of disability-related court cases that have been decided since mid-2017, even with the tougher requirement that schools ensure that students with disabilities make appropriate progress from year to year. But there are signs that schools are settling *Endrew-F.-*like cases in favor of the student. Of course, the number of cases decided by a judge is miniscule compared to the millions of school-based actions and decisions related to students with disabilities every year. So, the most important changes may be happening at the school level.

In recent years, there have been cases involving the right of students with disabilities to participate in team sports (see *Bingham v. Oregon School Activities Association*), to accessible school websites (see *Marcie Lipsitt v. Spokane Public Schools*), and to accommodations for food allergies (see *T.F. v. Fox Chapel Area School District*). These are important developments that may affect thousands of schools around the country.

GETTING MORE INFORMATION

Here's a list of mostly national-level organizations that can provide more in-depth information on educating students with disabilities. This list is not exhaustive. You may also wish to look up state and local resources, including resources offered by your own school district.

- American Association of People with Disabilities: https://www.aapd.com
- Disability.gov: https://www.dol.gov/odep/topics/disability.htm
- LDOnline: http://www.ldonline.org/index.php
- National Association of Special Education Teachers: https://www.naset.org
- National Disability Rights Network: www.ndrn.org
- U.S. Department of Education IDEA website: https://sites.ed.gov/idea/

San Antonio Independent School District v. Rodriguez (1973)

Children do not have a fundamental right under the U.S. Constitution to a public education.

When the Founding Fathers deliberated over what rights people in a free nation ought to have, they came up with a formidable list, including freedom of speech and religion, a trial by jury, due process, protection against search and seizure of our home or belongings, and even the right to a "well-regulated militia." Nowhere in the Bill of Rights, however, appear other items that we might consider indispensable today: a home, for instance, or access to a doctor, or a job. Or, for that matter, a high-quality education for our children.

To the extent we desire such things, they are for the free market and our elected officials to provide and are subject in key ways to our ability to afford them. To be sure, the U.S. Supreme

Court has, over the years, determined that we have a fundamental right to educate our own children as we see fit—for example, to homeschool them for religious reasons or send them to private school. But what of public education itself? Do children have a right to *any* public education, much less a high-quality education, or one that is substantially equal for all children regardless of what neighborhood they live in or their race or family income? It is these questions that the Court grappled with in the *Rodriguez* case.

Demetrio Rodriguez was born to a migrant-farm-working family. He was a veteran who served in World War II and the Korean War. He served in the Navy and the Air Force Reserve and was employed at the Kelly Air Force Base as a sheet-metal worker. He and wife, Belen, had five children—David, Alex, Carlos, Patricia, and James.

Demetrio's children resided in and attended the Edgewood School District in Texas. In 1968, the schools in the Edgewood district were crumbling; classrooms were overcrowded and lacked basic school supplies; few guidance counselors worked there; and a substantial percentage of teachers were not properly certified to teach students. That spring, four hundred students walked out of Edgewood High School to protest substandard educational facilities at their school.

Demetrio's son Alex recalls his elementary school's leaky windows, its lack of air-conditioning, and its condemned third floor—which, incidentally, didn't stop class from being held there.

The conditions upset Demetrio, who wanted his five children to have a decent education, especially since he had had to quit school after the sixth grade.

He teamed up with other Mexican American parents to do something about it. They soon learned that it wasn't the school district itself; it was the state that was not providing enough money. And there wasn't much the local district could do to fill the deficit; the Edgewood district could raise only $50 per student from property taxes while the wealthier Alamo Heights district could raise $500 per student.

Historically, funding for Texas public schools was structured such that 10 percent came from the federal government, 50 percent came from a duo of state education funds (20 percent of which actually came from local sources), and 40 percent from local governments in the form of taxation on homeowners' property taxes. Therefore, as in most school districts across the nation, the funding of public education in Texas was (and is) heavily dependent on revenue derived from local taxation.

THE CASE

Demetrio Rodriguez helped to form an association of Mexican American parents who eventually became plaintiffs in a class action lawsuit on behalf of themselves and other minority and poor children residing in resource-poor school districts throughout Texas.

Here was the situation they presented to the courts.

In the late 1960s, Edgewood was one of seven public school districts in the San Antonio metropolitan area. Some 22,000 students were enrolled in its twenty-five elementary and secondary schools. Approximately 90 percent of the student population was Mexican American; 6 percent was African American. The average assessed property value per pupil was $5,960; the median family income was $4,686 per year. The per-pupil annual school expenditure in the district was typically $356.

In contrast, the nearby Alamo Heights school district enrolled 5,000 students, of which more than 80 percent were white. The assessed property value per pupil was $49,078, and the median family income was $8,001. The per-pupil annual school expenditure in the district was typically $594.

The case made its way to the U.S. Supreme Court, which, in a 5 to 4 vote, ruled in 1973 that education is not a fundamental right under the U.S. Constitution and that Texas' scheme of financing its schools was not irrational or discriminatory.

MAKING HISTORY

Demetrio Rodriguez's fight for equal educational opportunity spanned decades.

Although he did not prevail in the U.S. Supreme Court, Demetrio persisted, eventually securing a victory on behalf of Edgewood district students in Texas state court in 1984.

Demetrio's children marvel at their father's fighting spirit that led to the Supreme Court case that now bears their surname. "He wasn't just thinking about me and my brothers at that time. He was thinking about . . . future kids," said son Alex.

"He was my hero," said daughter Patricia, who became a third-grade bilingual teacher in the Edgewood district. "I would like for other people to remember him as a great warrior. Even though he wasn't well educated, he didn't let that stop him. It didn't keep him from fighting for what he thought was right."

Patricia believes that her father's efforts boiled down to the "same basic idea that all schools should be funded equally based not on what side of town you live on or how much your house is worth. It's how much is your children's education worth."

THE DECISION

The Court held that Texas' scheme of distributing state education funds to school districts according to a complex formula and requiring local governments to supply the rest through local property taxes was rationally related to the state's interest in providing for public education and did not violate the Equal Protection Clause of the U.S. Constitution.

In reaching this conclusion, the Court made several other important determinations. First, it concluded that unequal school conditions based on the income of students and families did not warrant heightened scrutiny by courts. "At least where wealth is involved, the Equal Protection Clause does not require absolute equality or precisely equal advantages," the Court stated.

Second, it concluded that public education is not a "fundamental" right or interest under the U.S. Constitution that would require courts to scrutinize inequalities in public schools much more closely. "Education, of course, is not among the rights afforded explicit protection under our Federal Constitution. Nor do we find any basis for saying it is implicitly so protected," said the Court.

The Court stated that it had to decide "whether the Texas system of financing public education operates to the disadvantage of some suspect class or impinges upon a fundamental right explicitly or implicitly protected by the Constitution, thereby requiring strict judicial scrutiny. If so, the judgment of the [lower court, which had

IN FACT

Even after controlling for variations between states that affect education spending, there are wide disparities in funding among states. In 2015, funding levels ranged from a high of $18,719 per pupil in New York, to a low of $6,277 per pupil in Idaho. (This means that, in 2015, the average student in Idaho had access to only one-third of the funding available to a similar student in New York.) States also treat their poorest districts very differently. Utah, for example, gives more than 40 percent *additional* funds to its high-poverty school districts compared to its low-poverty districts, whereas Nevada does the opposite, giving more than 40 percent *fewer* funds to its high-poverty districts than to its low-poverty districts.

decided in favor of the plaintiffs] should be affirmed." The Court located neither a suspect class nor a fundamental right in this case; as a result, the plaintiffs lost the case.

Important Concepts

Suspect Class

In federal constitutional law, a suspect class is a classification or categorization of people according to some trait or attribute that raises a serious judicial eyebrow (so to speak). Race is a suspect class, as is sex or gender. Thus, if a government policy or system differentiates people by race or gender, the courts have, in effect, said, "Hey, government! That's serious. You've got to justify what you're doing here, and we are not going to defer and assume what you're doing is legitimate."

Actually, the plaintiffs in the *Rodriguez* case did raise race as a factor in the government's school funding scheme; they alleged that the racial minority children concentrated in poor school districts were discriminated against compared to white children. But, despite the fact that students in resource-poor schools in Texas were overwhelmingly racial minorities, the Supreme Court largely sidestepped the issue of race in its opinion, focusing instead on whether wealth was a suspect class. Its answer: *nope*. (This answer tells us much about how huge income inequalities can be tolerated in a democratic nation that prides itself on freedom and equality.)

The problem was that the *Rodriguez* Court couldn't figure out how to define a discrete class of Texas children on the basis of wealth. Should it focus on all children in non-rich school districts? Or only children in school districts with property values below a certain level? What about poor children attending rich school districts?

In the end, the Court threw up its hands and concluded:

> [I]t is clear that [plaintiffs ask] this Court . . . to review a system that allegedly discriminates against a large, diverse, and amorphous class, unified only by the common factor of residence in districts that happen to have less taxable wealth than other districts. [This] class is not saddled with such disabilities, or

subjected to such a history of purposeful unequal treatment, or relegated to such a position of political powerlessness as to command extraordinary protection from the majoritarian political process. We thus conclude that the Texas system does not operate to the peculiar disadvantage of any suspect class.

Fundamental Right

The classification of a right as fundamental restricts the ability of the federal, state, or local government to limit it. Courts determine whether rights are fundamental by examining whether they are part of a longstanding history or tradition in the United States.

In *Rodriguez*, the plaintiffs argued that education is a fundamental right because it is essential to utilizing other cherished rights, such as free speech or the right to vote. With this argument, the Court spied a slippery slope: "How," it asked, "is education to be distinguished from the significant personal interests in the basics of decent food and shelter?"

The Court concluded: "Nothing this Court holds today in any way detracts from our historic dedication to public education. But [its] importance . . . does not determine whether it must be regarded as fundamental."

And there you have it: Education, according to our highest court, is not a fundamental right under our federal Constitution.

IMPLICATIONS FOR EDUCATORS AND SCHOOLS

- The *Rodriguez* case is generally seen as a devastating setback for public education. Realistically, however, even had plaintiffs won the case, it is unlikely that the Supreme Court would have dictated what it means for states to provide a high-quality education for every student—that would have involved too many variables and is something over which courts have no expertise. On the other hand, the Court was one vote away from ruling that Texas had not provided enough for students in poor districts; that alone would have had a seismic effect on states and districts nationwide.

- The *Rodriguez* case highlights the fact that school funding comes from all three levels of government. Every state has a different ratio of federal, state, and local funds. For example, in 2014–2015, the percentages of total school revenues coming from federal, state, and local sources in Illinois were 8 percent, 25 percent, and 67 percent, respectively, while the corresponding total revenues in Vermont were 6 percent, 90 percent, and 4 percent. That's quite a difference. And in Illinois, local property taxes provided 59 percent of all school funds, whereas in Vermont that figure was *zero* percent! These variations reflect a crazy patchwork system of public education funding across the United States. So, if you're wondering where to direct your advocacy (or your ire), it helps to know which level of government is most responsible for any shortfalls your school or district is experiencing.

Reflection

In the landmark case, *Brown v. Board of Education*, the Supreme Court, in outlawing racial segregation in schools, recognized the importance of education to our democratic society. "[Education] is the very foundation of good citizenship," the Court said, and "it is doubtful that any child may reasonably be expected to succeed in life if he is denied the opportunity of an education," which "is a right which must be made available to all on equal terms." Yet, less than twenty years later, the Court in *Rodriguez* struck a very different tone in deciding that the disparity between predominantly Mexican American schools with few resources and mostly white schools with ample resources did not violate a fundamental right or anything in the U.S. Constitution. How has *Rodriguez* impacted your school district? What does equal educational opportunity mean? How might you teach the *Brown* case differently in light of *Rodriguez*?

GETTING PROACTIVE

School funding may seem like a distant and unwinnable fight for educators who, along with students, bear the brunt of insufficient and inequitably distributed resources. Fair enough. But it turns out that educators do have influence; many politicians and policymakers who control the purse strings are much more likely to consider the opinion of an educator (who can describe firsthand what resources they lack and what that means for students) than that of an advocate or lobbyist who is not directly affiliated with a school.

If you're inclined to raise your voice on school funding, the first step is to get informed: How does your school or district compare to other schools or districts in your state? And how does your state compare to other states? Here are some places to look for answers:

> Under the Every Student Succeeds Act (ESSA)—the federal law that replaced No Child Left Behind—states are now required to publish online, annually, the per-pupil spending for each *school* and *district* in the state. Reported expenditures must include actual teacher salaries, which make up the majority of most school budgets. This greatly enhanced level of data can help with comparisons between schools and districts in your state. To find this data, check out your state education department's website.

> A number of researchers have developed state-by-state comparisons of school funding, according to certain criteria (for example, the overall per-pupil funding provided, the degree to which funds are especially directed to resource-poor districts, and the funding provided relative to overall state revenue). See "Getting More Information."

> Share with policymakers how education funding affects your classroom. Mention specific resources that you need

or lack. Don't forget to specify what you pay out of your own pocketbook. (Research shows that teachers spend on average $500 a year on school supplies.) Your stories can help elected leaders understand that funding matters to students, parents, teachers—and voters.

Classroom AND Community VOICES

Public Elementary School Teacher
Kentucky

As a teacher who has worked in three different states, I have witnessed how school districts' reliance on local property taxes causes great disparity in school programs and facilities. Kentucky, where I currently teach, passed the landmark Kentucky Education Reform Act (KERA) in 1990, which created a complex funding formula that guaranteed a minimum amount of money that each school district would receive from the state each year. However, the Kentucky state legislature has not approved any significant increases to school funding since 2008, and the continued reliance on local property taxes for a portion of school funding has caused the disparity to grow between rich and poor counties. Although there is no specific wording in the U.S. Constitution about education, this funding gap seems to run counter to the general principles in the Preamble to "establish justice" and "promote the general welfare." Given that the U.S. Supreme Court voted 5 to 4 in the *Rodriguez* case shows that the school funding issue is in no way a "closed case." It is bound to come up again in the future!

Alex Corbitt
Middle School English Teacher, New York

The *Rodriguez* ruling was reached after the court found that funding disparities between school districts do not disadvantage any particular suspect class. In my experience, this is untrue. For example, in New York City, our nation's most segregated school system, a family's zip code is a significant indicator of students' income and ethnicity. The *de facto* segregation throughout the city is linked to a long history of systemic redlining and housing discrimination. Without significant equitable funding efforts from federal, state, and local government, students of color, who attend schools funded largely through local property taxes, would be even more disproportionately deprived of school resources than they are now.

Also, equitable funding does not guarantee appropriate resources. My classroom library was barren when I began teaching middle school literacy in the Bronx. Over the next two years, I visited book drives around New York and New Jersey and accumulated over one thousand books for my classroom library. I slowly realized, however, that the books I purchased featured predominantly white, middle-class protagonists. These books were not culturally relevant to my black and Latinx students. I subsequently learned how to better listen to my students, find books that matched their interests, and write grants to fund a more culturally relevant classroom library.

RECENT DEVELOPMENTS

After *Rodriguez*, while school funding cases invoking federal law occasionally pop up, the vast majority of litigation related to inadequate or inequitable school funding now occurs in state courts. Many state constitutions have provisions establishing a duty of the state to provide for public education that is, for example, "general," "thorough," "common," "uniform," "sufficient," "free," "efficient," "complete," "high quality," or "suitable." In recent years, several state courts (for example, Kansas and New Mexico) have concluded that the system of school finance violates the state's constitution; but others (for example, Connecticut and Texas) have held the opposite.

- One notable exception to the slew of state cases is *Gary B. v. Snyder*, a federal case in which a group of students attending Detroit public schools argued that their schools are so underfunded and mismanaged by the state of Michigan that their condition denies students a right of access to literacy under the U.S. Constitution. Although the federal judge in the case agreed that literacy is vitally important to public life—and that the conditions in Detroit public schools are "devastating"—he concluded that the U.S. Constitution does not demand that Michigan "affirmatively provide each child with a defined, minimum level of education by which the child can attain literacy." As of Fall 2019, the case is still pending in the federal appellate court.

GETTING MORE INFORMATION

Here's a list of mostly national-level organizations, publications, and databases that can provide more in-depth information on school funding. This list is not exhaustive. You may also wish to look up state and local resources, including research and data made available by your own school district.

- Center on Budget and Policy Priorities: visit https://www.cbpp.org (see "state budget and tax")
- Civil Rights Data Collection: https://ocrdata.ed.gov (see "staffing and finance" under school or district searches)
- The Education Trust: https://edtrust.org (see "funding equity")

- Education Week: https://www.edweek.org (see "Quality Counts" school finance reports)
- Learning Policy Institute: https://learningpolicyinstitute.org (see "equitable resources and access")
- National Center for Education Statistics: https://nces.ed.gov (see "Education Finance Statistics Center")
- National Conference of State Legislatures: http://www.ncsl.org (see "The state role in education finance")
- School Funding Fairness: http://www.schoolfundingfairness.org (see "Is School Funding Fair?: A National Report Card")
- School Funding Info: http://schoolfunding.info (see state-by-state updates on litigation)
- Shanker Institute/Rutgers Graduate School of Education: http://schoolfinancedata.org (see "annual report")
- Urban Institute: https://www.urban.org (see "school finance")

CASE 6

Lau v. Nichols (1974)

English learners* are entitled to equal educational opportunity and a meaningful education.

I was born in the United States, just a few years after my parents immigrated from South Korea. They almost opted to move to San Francisco, where the *Lau v. Nichols* case originated and which had a military base at the time. (My dad was a doctor who got fast-track citizenship by working in the U.S. military.) But they went to Pennsylvania instead, and soon afterward settled in what was then a relatively rural part of New Jersey where no one looked like me, much less spoke Korean.

---

*I use the term "English learner" or "EL" for students learning the English language because it's the term predominantly used in law and policy today. Until quite recently, the most commonly used term was "Limited English Proficient" or "LEP" student. Today, many educators prefer terms like "emergent bilingual" or "emerging bilingual" that more accurately describe EL students' language ability and educational path.

My parents decided they would raise me speaking English only. I attended an almost all-white school with no English learner (EL) program or population. I wonder what would have happened if my public school had been equipped to educate a bilingual or multilingual child? What if I had lived somewhere where the majority of kids spoke another language at home?

What if I had been Kinney Lau?

Kinmon "Kinney" Lau was born in Hong Kong. In 1969, when Kinney was five, he and his mother moved to San Francisco, where they were later joined by his father, a carpenter. Kinney attended Jean Parker Elementary School, near San Francisco's Chinatown, where nearly every student was of Chinese descent.

He spoke little English and received no specialized English language or bilingual instruction at school.

At the time, of the 2,856 students of Chinese ancestry in San Francisco's school system who did not speak English, only one thousand were afforded supplemental courses in the English language. (Even by 1973, years after the *Lau* case was filed, less than half of the Chinese students needing special English instruction in San Francisco were receiving it.)

California law stated that "English shall be the basic language of instruction in all schools" and that it is "the policy of the state" to ensure "the mastery of English by all pupils in the schools." In fact, the state forbade students who did not meet the standards of proficiency in English from receiving a high school diploma.

Edward Steinman was an advocate working in the Chinatown office of the San Francisco Neighborhood Legal Assistance Foundation in the late 1960s. Steinman happened to be representing Kinney's mother, Kam Wai Lau, in a landlord-tenant dispute. He knew that she and her son spoke no English and that Kinney had no access to special language programs at school. He asked Ms. Lau to have her son participate in a class-action lawsuit against the school district; she agreed. Kinney Lau's name was placed first in a list of thirteen plaintiffs in the suit that became *Lau v. Nichols*.

MAKING HISTORY

The *Lau* case put a spotlight on the needs of English learners in U.S. public schools.

Few would argue with the importance of the *Lau* decision in changing the landscape for English learner students in San Francisco, which now offers a variety of bilingual and bicultural programs for thousands of ELs, and in other districts around the country, which adopted "Lau" plans to meet the needs of its limited- and non-English-speaking students.

Nevertheless, Kinney Lau—who now goes by "Ken" and speaks flawless English— is apparently a "reluctant poster child" for bilingual education, perhaps because he never benefited from it himself; even after he won in court, most of San Francisco's ESL and bilingual classes remained insufficient and poorly designed. By the time dual-language instruction was introduced, he was too old to receive it. So how did his English get so good? By watching American television, he said.

continues

But Lau appears to acknowledge the benefits of specialized instruction for other English learners. "If you throw [EL students] in the classroom and tell them to sink or swim, there's a much bigger probability that they're going to sink."

"The thing about America is that if you're not native Indian, then you're an immigrant by default," he said. "People risk so much to come here; I think they should be able to retain their language and their culture."

THE CASE

The Laus and other Chinese families sued the San Francisco Unified School District in 1970, charging that the district's language policy failed to provide appropriate language instruction to children in the district who spoke only Cantonese and violated both the students' rights to Equal Protection under the Fourteenth Amendment of the U.S. Constitution and Title VI of the Civil Rights Act of 1964.

The case made its way up to the U.S. Supreme Court, which, in 1974, unanimously held in favor of Lau and the other plaintiffs. The Court cited federal civil rights regulations specifying that "where inability to speak and understand the English language excludes national origin-minority group children from effective participation in the educational program offered by a school district, the district must take affirmative steps to rectify the language deficiency in order to open its instructional program to these students."

THE DECISION

The Supreme Court in January 1974 unanimously reversed the decision of the lower appellate court, which had ruled in favor of the San Francisco school district, holding that the school district

violated Title VI of the Civil Rights Act of 1964, a federal antidiscrimination statute, by not offering non-English-speaking students
any special programs to learn English and receive a meaningful
education. The Court chose not to address the plaintiffs' constitutional claim that the district violated their right to equal protection. The case was sent back to the lower court to determine an
appropriate course of action for San Francisco EL students impacted by the decision.

Title VI of the Civil Rights Act of 1964 prohibits discrimination based on race, color, or national origin in any program or
activity receiving federal financial assistance. All public schools
(and many private schools) receive federal aid and must comply
with Title VI as a condition of receiving that aid. Senator Hubert
Humphrey, during floor debates on the Civil Rights Act of 1964,
famously explained: "Simple justice requires that public funds,
to which all taxpayers of all races contribute, not be spent in any
fashion which encourages, entrenches, subsidizes, or results in
racial discrimination."

Important Concepts

The relevant federal civil rights regulations that the *Lau* Court
relied upon included one that directed districts to take affirmative
steps to aid students whose inability to speak and understand English excluded them from *effective participation* in the educational
program offered by a school district.

Effective Participation

One of the main challenges of educators of EL students is to ensure
that EL students do not lose out on years of learning in a variety of
domains and subjects while they also develop their English language skills. The Court in *Lau* seemed to harp on this point:

> *Basic English skills are at the very core of what these public
> schools teach. Imposition of a requirement that, before a child
> can* effectively participate *in the educational program, he must
> already have acquired those basic skills is to make a mockery of*

public education. (Emphasis added.) We know that those who do not understand English are certain to find their classroom experiences wholly incomprehensible and in no way meaningful.

And so *Lau* established that ELs must not be siloed into a kind of permanent, separate track of education; "effective participation" means they must be provided a "meaningful" opportunity to receive instruction and to engage in the classroom, just like other students. It also makes clear that education of ELs is not to be equated with (or limited to) English language instruction alone. Subsequent regulations and judicial decisions have reinforced and helped to enforce the concept of effective participation for ELs in curriculum and instruction.

IMPLICATIONS FOR EDUCATORS AND SCHOOLS

The Court did not specify in *Lau* what type of EL instruction or intervention would satisfy civil rights laws. That further direction has come from subsequent statutes, judicial opinions, and guidance.

- In the same year that the Court issued the *Lau* ruling, Congress enacted the Equal Educational Opportunities Act (EEOA), which requires states and public schools to take "appropriate action" to overcome language barriers that impede equal participation by students in their instructional programs.

- Then, six years after *Lau*, a federal appellate court articulated a process to determine whether schools' EL programs comply with civil rights laws. This process, which has been broadly adopted by other courts and by the federal government, consists of a three-part test (sometimes called the "*Castañeda*" test) for schools in assessing EL programs:

1. The educational theory underlying the language assistance program is recognized as sound by some experts in the field or is considered a legitimate experimental strategy;

2. The program and practices used by the school system are reasonably calculated to implement effectively the educational theory adopted by the school; and

3. The program succeeds, after a legitimate trial, in producing results indicating that students' language barriers are actually being overcome within a reasonable period of time.

● In 2015, the U.S. Departments of Education and Justice articulated ten specific items (and provided an accompanying toolkit, listed below) for schools to focus on to ensure equality for EL students:

1. Identify and assess all potential EL students accurately and in timely fashion.

2. Provide appropriate language assistance to EL students.

3. Provide sufficient resources to ensure EL programs are effectively implemented.

4. Provide ELs meaningful access to grade-level curricula and programs.

5. Conduct EL programs in the least segregative manner possible.

6. Provide EL students with disabilities with both language assistance and disability-related services.

7. Allow parents to opt children out of EL programs/ services but also monitor opt-out students.

8. Monitor the progress of all EL students; do not exit students from EL programs prematurely.

9. Evaluate EL programs over time, using accurate data, and modify EL programs when needed.

10. Communicate with limited-English-proficient parents in a language they can understand.

To underscore item 10 above: One of the most important skills for educators is engaging effectively with family members who speak languages other than English. Schools should provide appropriate written or oral translation of communications, including notices, meetings, conferences, events, and other school activities where parents and family members are given an opportunity to engage or participate. This is no small challenge, especially in communities where dozens or even hundreds of languages other than English may be spoken at home.

IN FACT

In 2015, 9.5 percent or 4.8 million students in the United States were English learners. Greater than 10 percent of students in Alaska, California, Colorado, Kansas, Nevada, New Mexico, Texas, and Washington were ELs. California was highest at 21 percent. Three out of four ELs and nearly 8 percent of all public K–12 students spoke Spanish at home. Arabic, Chinese, and Vietnamese were the next most common home languages.

Reflection

Consider this 2007 reflection by attorney Edward Steinman in the *Lau* case: "The *Lau* case has been around forever, but court cases are just a piece of paper. They're not self-executing. Even thirty something years after *Lau*, we still have millions of students who—because of no fault of their own—languish in classrooms where content may be incomprehensible." Does this observation ring true to you? How faithful to *Lau* is the EL program at your school?

GETTING PROACTIVE

Among the many important decisions educators must make in educating English learners, three critical junctures stand out: (1) correctly identifying who is an EL as soon as possible; (2) determining what instruction or program is appropriate for ELs; and (3) exiting ELs from specialized instruction at the right time.

- To identify potential ELs, ensure your school is effectively implementing a valid home language survey in relevant languages.

- Once students are identified as potential ELs, use a valid and reliable assessment (placement or screener tests) to determine if they are indeed ELs.

- Assess EL programs and services using the three-step *Castañeda* test (described earlier) and other evaluation techniques. Ensure that EL programs are designed to enable ELs to attain both English proficiency and equal participation in the school's standard instructional program within a reasonable length of time.

- Monitor and regularly assess the progress of ELs; use valid assessments and criteria to determine whether students are ready to exit EL programs and services; and continue to monitor students to determine whether they have exited prematurely.

Classroom AND Community VOICES

Liz Kleinrock
Elementary School Teacher, California

My school recently started administering the English Language Proficiency Assessments for California (ELPAC). In California, it's mandated that emerging bilingual (EB) students receive thirty minutes of direct language instruction per day, so my school created "academic clubs." The purpose of these clubs is to ensure that EB students are not pulled out of their classroom. We don't want them to miss out on activities that other students get to participate in. Every day for thirty minutes, we mix students across grades and classes for enrichment-based academics that target specific needs. We group EB students based on their ELPAC scores. For example, I currently teach a "Level 3" EB club through the lens of oral storytelling and use a curriculum provided by a popular storytelling podcast, alongside English Language Assessment standards, and guided by ELPAC data.

RECENT DEVELOPMENTS

Depending on how you look at it, a trio of legal developments have either (a) given schools a lot more breathing room to educate ELs as they see fit or (b) undermined the principle articulated in *Lau* that ELs must be afforded an equal and meaningful education.

- In 2001, in *Alexander v. Sandoval*, the Supreme Court held that individuals no longer have the right to sue under Title VI of the Civil Rights Act (as was the case in *Lau*) for actions that have the *effect* of harming English learners or other students on the basis of race or national origin but do not amount to *intentional* discrimination. (Much of the basis for the *Lau* decision was not that school officials intended to harm English learners but that the effect or impact of its policies and practices caused harm.) Federal agencies, however, still have the ability to enforce Title VI against schools for actions that have a discriminatory effect or impact.

- In 2009, in *Horne v. Flores*, the Supreme Court held that, under the Equal Educational Opportunities Act (enacted by Congress in 1974), "appropriate action" by school districts does not necessarily require any particular level of funding for EL services or instruction and that states and school districts should be given latitude as to whether they are taking "appropriate action" with respect to EL services and instruction.

- In 2015, the Every Student Succeeds Act (ESSA), which replaced the No Child Left Behind Act (NCLB), was enacted by Congress. ESSA provides grants to states and districts for EL programs; it also requires states and districts to assess the progress of English learners in English language proficiency as well as in math, reading, and science. However, states and districts have much more autonomy under ESSA than under NCLB as to how or when to impose reforms when ELs fail to make academic progress in particular schools.

GETTING MORE INFORMATION

Here's a list of national-level organizations that provide more in-depth information or further resources on educating English learners. This list is not exhaustive. You may also wish to look up state and local resources, including resources offered by your own school district.

- Colorín Colorado, www.colorincolorado.org
- Migration Policy Institute, www.migrationpolicy.org
- National Association for Bilingual Education, www.nabe.org

- National Clearinghouse for English Language Acquisition, https://ncela.ed.gov

- U.S. Department of Education, www.ed.gov (see "English Learner Tool Kit," "Civil Rights Obligations to English Learner Students," and "ESSA Guidance on English Learners and Title III Programs")

CASE 7

Tinker v. Des Moines Independent Community School District (1969)

Students' free-speech rights must be respected unless the speech substantially interferes with school operations.

"The Times They Are a-Changin" was written by Bob Dylan in 1964—a song, if there ever was one, that captures an era. To this Gen-X-er, the swelling and sometimes violent student protests of the 1960s and early 1970s seem both remarkable and foreign. I was not of this era; I came of age in the late 1970s and 1980s, in a relatively privileged community in which examples of free speech were infrequent and not all that riveting. (The biggest school protest I recall surrounded whether a sixth-grade production of *West Side Story* should be allowed; the answer was no.)

Today, students—especially college students—are making themselves heard around issues of, for example, police misconduct, race and criminal justice, sexual assault, LGBTQ rights, and immigration. They owe much of their freedom to speak their mind to a considerably younger cohort of students: high schoolers like Mary Beth Tinker who grew up during the civil rights era, in the shadow of the Vietnam War.

Mary Beth Tinker was born in 1952 and grew up in Iowa. Her father was a Methodist minister. Her parents, who later became Quakers, believed that religious ideals should be put into action. The whole family became involved in the civil rights movement in the 1960s; one of Mary Beth's early memories is of her parents going to Mississippi in 1964 as part of Freedom Summer to register African Americans to vote.

Mary Beth's teenage years coincided with the Vietnam War. By 1965, about 170,000 U.S. soldiers were stationed in Vietnam. Graphic war footage appeared daily on television. As a thirteen-year-old student in eighth grade, Mary Beth was strongly affected by news of the war. She and her older brother John attended public schools in Des Moines, Iowa.

In December 1965, a group of adults and students in Des Moines, including the Tinkers, attended a meeting at the home of Christopher Eckhardt, another student in the district. The group was determined to publicize its objections to the hostilities in Vietnam and support for a truce by wearing black armbands during the holiday season (including at school) and by fasting on December 16 and New Year's Eve.

The principals of the Des Moines schools became aware of the plan to wear armbands. On December 14, 1965, they met and adopted a policy that any student wearing an armband to school would be asked to remove it, and students who refused would be suspended until they returned without the armband.

On December 16, Mary Beth Tinker and Christopher Eckhardt wore black armbands to their schools. John Tinker wore his armband the next day. They were all sent home and suspended from school until they would come back without their armbands. They did not return to school until after the planned period for wearing armbands had expired—after New Year's Day.

THE CASE

Represented by the ACLU, the students and their families embarked on a four-year court battle that culminated in the landmark Supreme Court decision that bears the Tinker family name.

Students and parents filed a civil rights action in federal court seeking to restrain the school officials and the board of directors of the school district from disciplining the students. The lower courts ruled in favor of the school district.

On February 24, 1969, the U.S. Supreme Court reversed in favor of the students, holding that their free speech rights had been improperly denied by the school district.

MAKING HISTORY

Mary Beth Tinker (right) with her brother, Paul, and mother, Lorena.

Today, Mary Beth Tinker is an advocate for the rights of youth, particularly in the areas of health and education. She is a retired pediatric nurse and holds master's degrees in public health and nursing.

She has observed a gradual erosion of free speech rights since 1969. "I think the political climate in the country discourages young people from speaking up," she says. "In a democracy, the people who are affected by decisions are supposed to be the ones who have the right to speak on their own behalf, and this should include young people . . . I think it's a big mistake in a democracy to discourage people from being involved in the democratic process, in whatever form that may take."

She continues to urge students to celebrate their right to speak out.

"Without encouraging a climate where free speech and dissidents' voices flourish," she says, "we won't benefit as much as we could as a society."

THE DECISION

The Supreme Court ruled against the Des Moines school district, upholding the students' First Amendment right of free speech expression. The Court famously stated, "It can hardly be argued that either students or teachers shed their constitutional rights to freedom of speech or expression at the schoolhouse gate." The Court also held that "where there is no finding and no showing that engaging in the forbidden conduct would materially and substantially interfere with the requirements of appropriate discipline in the operation of the school, the prohibition cannot be sustained."

Important Concepts
Material and Substantial Interference

The key question raised by the *Tinker* case—and asked by thousands of school administrators ever since—is whether a particular exercise of student speech would "materially and substantially interfere" with school activities or operations. What qualifies as "material and substantial interference"?

From the case itself, we know that, at minimum, it means something more than student speech or behavior that is merely uncomfortable or annoying. In order for school officials to justify prohibition of a particular expression of opinion, the Court said, they must be able to show something more than a "mere desire to

IN FACT

In a 2016 nationwide survey of high school students and teachers, 91 percent of students and 95 percent of teachers agreed that "people should be allowed to express unpopular opinions." But only 45 percent of those students and 53 percent of those teachers believed that people should be allowed to express "offensive" opinions (which in many cases are also protected by the First Amendment).

avoid the discomfort and unpleasantness that always accompany an unpopular viewpoint."

Nor is *fear* of a disturbance enough to prohibit the student speech. As the Court noted, "[a]ny word spoken, in class, in the lunchroom, or on the campus, that deviates from the views of another person may start an argument or cause a disturbance. But our Constitution says we must take this risk . . . it is this sort of hazardous freedom . . . that is the basis of our national strength and of [our] relatively permissive, often disputatious, society."

Here are some other signs or actions that the Court hinted *could* constitute material and substantial interference:

- Indication that the work of the school or any class was disrupted

- Threats or acts of violence on school premises

- Disturbances or disorders on the school premises

- Interruption of school activities

- Intrusion into school affairs or the lives of others

IMPLICATIONS FOR EDUCATORS AND SCHOOLS

- The case makes clear that free speech rights of students extend beyond the classroom itself to other areas of the school campus. In fact, students' free speech rights are arguably greater outside the classroom itself (but within school boundaries or at school-sponsored events) than within the classroom.

- One of the biggest lessons of the *Tinker* case for schools is that the manner and content of student speech are critical to determining whether it can be silenced or not. The Court distinguished the scenario in *Tinker* (wearing armbands to protest the Vietnam War) from other types of speech involving aggressive or disruptive actions, group demonstrations, interference with school operations, or the right of other students to be secure and to be let alone—all of which may be more easily stopped by schools.

- The Court also distinguished this case, involving a specific example of student expression, from other regulations or policies involving clothing or grooming. General regulations involving appearance or dress codes have been upheld by courts.

Reflection

Consider that unpopular, distasteful, or even upsetting and offensive speech that is not disruptive to school operations or invasive of others' rights is protected by the First Amendment, while verbal bullying or harassment (see Case 1) is not. How do you distinguish between offensive speech and bullying/harassment? How does your response differ depending on which scenario you encounter?

GETTING PROACTIVE

When I was an ACLU attorney, I frequently recited the mantra, "The best response to speech . . . is speech." In other words, in the vast majority of instances, when students hear speech that offends them or that they vehemently disagree with, instead of seeking to censor the opponent's voice, they need to develop the verbal and written skills (and the confidence and courage) to counter with their own speech. Why was what the other person said hurtful? How is that person's message ill-conceived, ignorant, or just plain wrong? What is an effective counter-narrative to that speech?

To be sure, the "fight speech with speech" mantra may seem unfair or unrealistic to some, especially for racially isolated or other marginalized student populations who experience some speech or speakers as hostile toward them or as targeting them. That said, educators play as central a role in promoting free speech itself as they do in developing the skills students need to communicate effectively. Peruse the resources at the end of the chapter to help you:

- Conduct a lesson on free speech and the U.S. Constitution.

- Educate students about offensive and hurtful speech, bias, and cyber-bullying—ideally *before* they happen, and especially *after* they happen.

Classroom AND Community VOICES

Tricia Ebarvia
High School English Teacher, Pennsylvania

In April of 2018, students across the country organized a national school walkout to show their support for the victims of the Parkland school shooting and to call for greater attention to gun safety laws. At my high school, hundreds of students planned to participate. However, if students walked out of class, they would have technically cut class, as per school policy, and receive disciplinary action.

Many students felt that such discipline violated their right to exercise free speech. What they failed to appreciate was the impact of their actions; it would cause instruction to stop, and students could potentially be unsupervised after leaving class. Ultimately, the administration and students worked together to come to a solution to minimize the disruption to the school, but the conflict offered a valuable opportunity for students to understand that free speech was not entirely unlimited. There are rights and responsibilities that come with free speech. It's important to consider all the stakeholders.

When we discuss potentially contentious issues, I ask students to generate a list of other individuals who have a stake in this issue. Then we consider how each of these individuals might view this particular issue, and more importantly, why.

For example, when we discussed the issue of gun safety following the Parkland shooting, we considered the perspectives of individuals such as students, parents, administrators, gun lobbyists, legislators, the news media, and many others. By asking students to think about an issue from the points of view of many stakeholders, especially those who may have different life experiences from their own, they are better able to imagine and anticipate the potential impact of their own speech.

High School Principal
Pennsylvania

I had a student named Roberto (not his real name), who decided that he would like to dress and present as a girl or young woman. We met as a faculty to discuss Roberto's wishes and decided that we needed to support him wholeheartedly. We wanted to live our values and have a school where all students felt safe to be who they are. We also wanted our school community to respect, accept, and support one another.

We decided to communicate directly with students and parents. We spent in-class time talking about LGBTQ issues, gender identity, personal expression, personal freedoms, dignity, and the importance of safe spaces for everyone. We also talked about violence against LGBTQ individuals and how destructive violence like this was not only to the victims, but also to the community at large. We showed students how hate destroys lives and communities and degrades all of us in the process. We sent emails to families about these conversations and included our school policies on student behavior, respect, and dignity (along with our school's dress code). We called parents who we thought might have concerns and invited them in to school to meet with us.

A week later Roberto came to school early and changed into a stereotypically female appearance, including wearing a dress. He asked that we refer to him as "Roberta" and use female pronouns.

Everything went smoothly; Roberta was warmly received. The best part of the day for me was toward the end of the day. Roberta strode through the hallway during our seventh-period switch, and she rushed to get to her next class; it felt like any other day. I learned that, in many ways, the adults in our community had more "baggage" and "hang-ups" about Roberta than the students did. I also learned that the ability to express one's identity is a critical component of free speech.

RECENT DEVELOPMENTS

Since *Tinker*, several prominent cases have arguably narrowed free speech protections for students. In some ways, judicial rulings mirror societal trends and attitudes. As you read the descriptions, consider that, since 1969, student fervor over the Vietnam War has subsided; the United States government embarked on a "War on Drugs"; school violence and mass school shootings have increased and received heightened attention; and millions of students (particularly students of color and students with disabilities) have been suspended or expelled from school or referred to law enforcement for engaging in "willful defiance" and other non-criminal behavior at school.

- In 1986, the Supreme Court said in *Bethel School District No. 403 v. Fraser* that the First Amendment does not prevent a school from prohibiting student speech that would undermine the school's basic educational mission; here, a student gave a sexually explicit speech with vulgar language and lewd conduct during an assembly attended by other students who were also minors.

- In 1988, the Court said in *Hazelwood School District v. Kuhlmeier* that, in the context of student speech in a school-sponsored publication (here, a school newspaper) that may be perceived to bear the "imprimatur" of the school, the school need not tolerate student speech that is inconsistent with its basic educational mission.

- In 2007, the Court held in *Morse v. Frederick* that school officials did not violate the First Amendment in disciplining a student who displayed a fourteen-foot banner bearing the phrase "BONG HiTs 4 JESUS" during the passing of the Olympic Torch Relay on a public street across the street from the school, where the speech could reasonably be regarded as "encouraging illegal drug use."

- In 2015, a federal appellate court held in *Bell v. Itawamba County School Board* that a student's rap recording—created off-campus and posted on Facebook and YouTube that contained threatening language against two school coaches and alluded to their sexual harassment of female students—reasonably could have been forecast to cause a substantial disruption of the school, and that therefore the student's suspension and placement in an alternative setting did not violate the First Amendment.

GETTING MORE INFORMATION

Here's a list of national-level organizations that provide more in-depth information or further resources on the First Amendment and free speech; encouraging challenging conversations in the classroom; and the intersection between free speech and bullying/harassment. This list is not exhaustive. You may also wish to look up state and local resources, including resources offered by your own school district.

- Anti-Defamation League, www.adl.org (see "A World of Difference" and "A Classroom of Difference")
- American Civil Liberties Union, www.aclu.org
- Annenberg Classroom, www.annenbergclassroom.org
- Free Speech Week, www.freespeechweek.org
- National Coalition Against Censorship, https://ncac.org
- Teaching Tolerance, www.tolerance.org (see "Mix It Up!")

CASE 8

Lee v. Weisman (1992)

Public schools may not persuade or compel a student to participate in a religious exercise or prayer.

s a student attending New Jersey public schools in the 1980s, I recited the Pledge of Allegiance every morning in homeroom before class began. One day, something changed. After the Pledge, our school instituted what was called a "moment of silence"—a minute or two during which we stood by our desks and watched the painfully slow progression of the minute hand on the wall clock, until the principal announced on the P.A. system that it was over. We weren't told the reason for the enforced silence, or what to think during it. Then, without warning, after a few months (or was it a few years?), the practice was halted, as suddenly as it had begun.

Years later, I learned that the New Jersey had passed a statute ostensibly to encourage "quiet and private contemplation and introspection," although the unspoken purpose, to some, was to facilitate student prayer. The statute was struck down by the courts in 1985. The moment of silence was my only firsthand experience with the commingling of church and state in public schools.

During roughly the same period as the "moment of silence" experiment in New Jersey, a different practice—yet one that raised similar concerns—had been taking place in Rhode Island.

It was 1986. Merith Weisman's graduation ceremony at Nathan Bishop Middle School was going smoothly—that is, until the Christian minister took the stage. Weisman is Jewish.

Public schools in Providence, Rhode Island, had a policy to permit school principals to invite members of the clergy to give invocations and benedictions at middle school and high school graduations.

Said father Daniel Weisman: "There was a benediction. We sat in the audience. At the end of the graduation, the minister asked everyone to stand and said please bow your heads. We are going to give a moment to thanks Jesus Christ for the accomplishment of your children."

"I was totally disarmed, humiliated, kind of stripped of my dignity at that moment, because that's not my religion. I'm not a Christian. And my identity, and part of who I am, is my religion, as a Jew who does not accept Christianity. And being forced to participate in a Christian ritual—and not being able to protect my family from also having to participate—it was almost like a rape, in a psychological sense. I felt diminished."

Daniel and Vivian Weisman called the school superintendent the next day to complain, arguing that graduation prayers violated the Constitution's guarantee of separation of church and state. They never received a response.

Fast forward three years. Now it was their younger daughter Deborah's turn to graduate. The Weismans decided to take up the issue of graduation prayer again with the school. Eventually, according to Daniel, a teacher on the faculty who was in charge of graduation found them to deliver "good news."

"She said [the school] was able to get a rabbi so we wouldn't be offended. We reminded her that was not what we were asking for. We appreciated her gesture . . . we did not want to be the oppressors of other people, parading our religion out in public for other people to have to be consumed, to be exposed to, having to deal with that, when that's not what they're there for."

The Weismans objected to the school principal, arguing that the rabbi's prayers could be offensive to some non-Jewish students at the school. More than half of the students in the Providence school system were black, Hispanic, or Asian. Many were Buddhist or Muslim.

Vivian Weisman thought the school system was being insensitive to the diversity of the student body. "We see prayer in public schools in any form as being very divisive. It really cuts out the minorities for whom the public school system has been a gateway for full inclusion in our society."

But the school district insisted on going ahead with the rabbi's prayer at graduation.

Four days before Deborah Weisman was to graduate from Nathan Bishop Middle School, Daniel Weisman sought a temporary restraining order in the U.S. District Court to prohibit school officials from including an invocation or benediction in the graduation ceremony. The court denied the motion for lack of adequate time to consider it.

Deborah and her family then attended the graduation, where Rabbi Leslie Gutterman, of the Temple Beth-El in Providence, delivered the following invocation prayer:

God of the Free, Hope of the Brave: For the legacy of America where diversity is celebrated and the rights of minorities are protected, we thank YOU. May these young men and women grow up to enrich it. For the liberty of America, we thank YOU. May these new graduates grow up to guard it. For the political process of America in which all its citizens may participate, for its court system where all may seek justice we thank YOU. May those we honor this morning always turn to it in trust. For the destiny of America we thank YOU. May the graduates of Nathan Bishop Middle School so live that they might help to share it. May our aspirations for our country and for these young people, who are our hope for the future, be richly fulfilled. AMEN.

MAKING HISTORY

Deborah Weisman (right) and her father, Daniel, respond to reporters' questions outside the U.S. Supreme Court. Listening are (from left) NPR correspondent Nina Totenberg, the Weismans' attorney Sandra Blanding, and BJC General Counsel Oliver S. Thomas.

When the Weismans filed suit, not everyone was on their side. School officials argued that the prayers are a matter of tradition for the city's schools. Daniel received negative attention at Rhode Island College, where he was on the faculty. Many of their friends were also unsupportive of the suit. The Weisman family received hate mail and telephone threats from people who felt they were anti-religion and anti-American. Many of Deborah's teachers and classmates disagreed with her stance (although over time some of them came to see the importance of the separation of church and state).

When the Supreme Court handed down its ruling, the Weismans were "surprised" and "thrilled" at their victory. But winning a major First Amendment case was perhaps not the most valuable civic lesson of the day for Deborah, who noted, "Even if we lost, I would have felt good because I have learned you can make a difference."

The Rabbi also led a benediction prayer expressing gratitude to "Lord" and "God" and asking for "blessing upon the teachers and administrators," and for "strength and guidance for graduates" as well as "help" for them to "understand that we are not complete with academic knowledge alone. We must each strive to fulfill what You require of us all: To do justly, to love mercy, to walk humbly."

THE CASE

In July 1989, with help from the American Civil Liberties Union, Daniel Weisman filed an amended complaint seeking to stop Providence public schools from inviting the clergy to deliver invocations and benedictions at future graduations.

The federal district and appellate courts agreed with the Weismans, and on June 24, 1992, the U.S. Supreme Court affirmed those rulings, holding that the First Amendment prohibits public schools from persuading or compelling a student to participate in a religious exercise at a graduation ceremony "where young graduates who object are induced to conform."

THE DECISION

In a close, 5 to 4 opinion, the Court held the prayer at the Rhode Island public school's graduation ceremony violated the Establishment Clause of the U.S. Constitution. The Court articulated what is now known as the "coercion test" to determine whether government is impermissibly *establishing or endorsing religion*.

"It is beyond dispute that, at a minimum, the Constitution guarantees that government may not coerce anyone to support or participate in religion or its exercise, or otherwise act in a way which establishes a [state] religion or religious faith, or tends to do so," said the Court.

The Court observed that the prayer exercises in this case were especially improper because the government (the public school) had "in every practical sense compelled attendance and participation" in an explicit religious exercise at an event that was so important that no student who objected had any choice but to attend anyway.

The Court held that the government can't "exact religious conformity" from students as a price of attending their own high school graduation.

Important Concepts

Establishment of Religion

The First Amendment of the U.S. Constitution states: "Congress shall make no law respecting an *establishment* of religion, or prohibiting the free exercise thereof" (emphasis added). In other words, in this nation, as the Court put it, "all creeds must be tolerated and none favored." *Lee v. Weisman* addresses the first clause of the sentence—the so-called Establishment Clause. (We'll examine the Free Exercise Clause later, in the *Mergens* case.)

In case you're wondering about how the First Amendment may apply to a local school district when it refers only to "Congress": by the middle of the twentieth century, the First Amendment (and most of the Bill of Rights) had been interpreted to apply not just to the federal government but to state and local governments as well.

Why do we have an Establishment Clause? (This would probably be a good to time for a history lesson, going back to the origins of the United States and even earlier—picture religious minorities fleeing Europe, various members of dominant and persecuted religions in the colonies, and sore feelings about the Church of England . . . okay, let's leave it there.) *Weisman* gives us some clues. As Justice Kennedy explained in the majority opinion, when the Constitution and Bill of Rights were being cobbled together, the Founding Fathers were not only concerned with the impact of government adoption of a dominant religion on religious minorities but on the "purity" of religion itself.

After all, Religion A would struggle to keep its integrity and good name if the government were to either foist it on resistant non-believers or water it down to be acceptable to followers of

Religion B or C. In this way, we can see how preventing the "establishment" of religion by government goes part and parcel with preserving the "free exercise" of religion.

It turns out that "lemon tests" are not just for buying used cars. In a famous case, *Lemon* v. *Kurtzman,* the Supreme Court came up with a three-part test to determine whether a government practice is impermissibly "establishing" a religion. Under that test, the government practice must (1) reflect a clearly secular or non-religious purpose; (2) have a primary effect that neither advances nor inhibits religion; and (3) avoid excessive government entanglement with religion. (Translation: A ceremony that includes a religious element held by a public school must not be designed to be religious, further or squelch anyone's religion, or cause the school to get tied up with a religious institution or enterprise.) This test is still cited often today when issues of separation of church and state arise.

The Court in *Weisman* appeared to address different parts of the *Lemon* test when it observed that the principal in Deborah's school went so far as to provide guidance to the rabbi as to how to deliver the prayer in a nonsectarian manner "to the point of creating a state-sponsored and state-directed religious exercise in a public school."

But in reality, the Court largely bypassed *Lemon* and focused

IN FACT

The *Weisman* case was not the first to address school prayer in public schools. In 1962, *Engel v. Vitale,* for example, the Court invalidated a New York public school prayer, "Almighty God, we acknowledge our dependence upon Thee, and we beg Thy blessings upon us, our parents, our teachers, and our Country," that was read aloud by each class in the presence of a teacher at the beginning of each school day. And in 1985 in *Wallace v. Jaffree,* the Court held that an Alabama statute authorizing a one-minute period of silence in all public schools for meditation or voluntary prayer violated the Establishment Clause.

instead on the coercive nature of school prayer at a graduation ceremony, where young students have no choice but to submit to religion in order to get their diploma. Recognizing that school graduation is one of "life's most significant occasions," the Court dismissed the school district's argument that, because the graduation ceremony was technically voluntary, students were not being coerced into religion.

IMPLICATIONS FOR EDUCATORS AND SCHOOLS

There's an interesting interplay between these two First Amendment edicts: one, the government may not prevent the *free exercise* of religion by individuals, and two, the government may not advance or *establish* a religion on its own. Here's how those principles operate in public schools:

- Suffice it to say that laws or policies that allow for adult-led, public-school-sanctioned prayer (or meditation or silence to enable prayer) are out.

- School prayer led by students, on the other hand, may be allowable. Indeed, schools are generally required to allow for student (or teacher) prayer on campus if students (or teachers) are acting on their own accord or as part of a voluntary, religion-themed group or club. Student-led prayer at school-sponsored events, however, may still be seen as coercive and therefore impermissible.

- In *Board of Education v. Mergens*, the Court held that student-led religious groups must be afforded equal access to school facilities if the school has opened up facilities to other non-curricular groups. The Court ruled similarly in the *Lamb's Chapel* and *Good News Club* cases with respect to after-school religious clubs and community-based religious clubs.

- Engaging in religion and teaching about religion are two different things. Schools can do the latter, not the former. (More on this later.)

Reflection

Some people believe that the *Weisman* case stopped a relatively benign practice of offering invocations or benedictions during school ceremonies that were more civic in nature than religious. Others agree with *Weisman* that children should not be made to follow or acquiesce to any religious exercise in public school. What do you think? Does the content of the prayer make a difference in whether it should be allowed or not?

GETTING PROACTIVE

True confession: I am a bit of a civil liberties purist. I don't necessarily like situations that blur the separation between church and state. For example, I didn't support the 2002 ruling in *Zelman v. Simmons-Harris*, in which the Supreme Court held that giving vouchers in the form of public school funds to parents to send children to private, parochial schools did not violate the Establishment Clause. I also disfavor intolerance toward students and teachers (as long as they are not attempting to proselytize or engage in religion with students) who happen to express themselves religiously through their appearance or words at school. Being a civil liberties purist means supporting *both* the rights of devout religious worshippers *and* those who wish to be free from religious influence in public spaces.

For me, therefore, getting proactive about religion and public schools means engaging on the topic from both sides of the coin:

- Teach the *Weisman* and *Santa Fe* (see page 96) cases, which struck down prayer in public schools. Then, teach the trio of Supreme Court cases mentioned earlier—*Mergens, Lamb's*

Chapel, and *Good News Club*—that uphold the free exercise of religion and equal treatment for religious community/student groups on school property.

- Consider whether religion is taught in your school in ways that are constitutional—that is, in a neutral manner that does not promote or privilege one religion over another and does not include actual prayer or practice in the curriculum. Are there valid ways to teach about world religions or spiritual practices that foster a greater understanding of diverse cultures and belief systems and their role (both positive and negative) in history, culture, or literature? Or does including any religion in the curriculum inevitably lead to privileging some religions over others?

Classroom AND Community VOICES

Parents of Middle and High School Students
Pennsylvania

We are Muslims. We live in Pennsylvania, and because of the current socio-political atmosphere we have been presented with unique challenges at work and at our children's school. We wish the school would accommodate the mid-day prayer that Muslims observe. Prayer is a major tenet of Islam. In order for any school to be truly inclusive, we believe there should be written policy that specifically addresses the need to give students time for Muslim prayer.

We also believe schools should think about the biases implicit in the school calendar (classroom celebrations, Halloween parade, holidays) and seasonal concerts. When we attend the school's seasonal concerts, the songs usually reflect Judeo-Christian beliefs. There are no Muslim celebrations or songs. School holidays and in-school celebrations often reflect Judeo-Christian beliefs. There is no observance of any Muslim celebrations or events.

Actions speak loudly. When you plan celebrations or sing holiday songs, ask yourself who's being left out and what kind of message that sends to all students. When your school or district shares holiday calendars, think about which religious holidays are privileged and which are ignored. A school or district does not have to purposefully exclude people from certain religions to send the message that their religion and beliefs are not valued.

To generate a greater understanding and respect for diversity in schools and in the world, teachers can make time for classroom discussions about various religions and their philosophies and practices, especially in connection to the social studies curriculum. Administrators can rethink school traditions like concerts or holiday parties. What would it mean to make them truly inclusive?

RECENT DEVELOPMENTS

In 2000, in *Santa Fe Independent School District v. Doe*, the U.S. Supreme Court relied on *Weisman* in holding that student-led, student-initiated prayer at football games violated the Establishment Clause. Key to the decision were the fact that the prayer was delivered "on school property, at school-sponsored events, over the school's public address system, by a speaker representing the student body, under the supervision of school faculty, and pursuant to a school policy that explicitly and implicitly encourages public prayer."

- In 2018, Kentucky approved state academic standards for Bible literacy classes in public schools; the ACLU had voiced concern that the manner in which some of these classes had been taught in the state was too "devotional" and straight out of "Sunday school."

- Also, in 2018, a federal appellate court upheld a version of a student production of a "Christmas Spectacular" that featured references to multiple religions; previous versions of the production (that had been on shaky ground legally) had included an extended Christian nativity scene as well as students playing Biblical characters.

- The ACLU has represented several students in recent years who have been persecuted for expressing their religion at school—for example, a Muslim student who wore a kufi, a Sikh student who wore a turban and carried a kirpan, a Jewish student who wore a Star of David pendant, and Christian students who wished to read the Bible during free periods or wear rosaries, crosses, and other articles of faith.

GETTING MORE INFORMATION

Here's a list of national-level organizations that provide more in-depth information or further resources on the First Amendment and religion. This list is not exhaustive. You may also wish to look up state and local resources, including resources offered by your own school district.

- American Civil Liberties Union, www.aclu.org

- Americans United for the Separation of Church and State, https://www.au.org

- Freedom from Religion Foundation, https://ffrf.org

- People for the American Way, http://www.pfaw.org
- Religious Freedom Center, http://www.religiousfreedom center.org
- Religious Freedom Institute, https://www.religiousfreedom institute.org

Safford Unified School District No. 1 v. Redding (2009)

School officials may not conduct excessively intrusive searches of students.

*T*hese days, with school shootings happening almost daily and decades after the introduction of metal detectors to schools, the notion that students might have any rights at all not to be searched and inspected at any time for weapons seems almost quaint. But if we rewind thirty years or so, the bigger youth policy concern was not guns but drugs. This was the time of Nancy Reagan's "Just Say No" campaign. In the 1980s, the focus was on deterring (and criminalizing) crack and cocaine use. In more recent years, the drug of choice has included heroin, methamphetamines, inhalants, and prescription medications. Today, opioid abuse has reached epidemic levels in many communities. The duty to keep students safe from drugs and weapons remains squarely on the shoulders of educators and school administrators. The question becomes: What remains of students' right to privacy over their belongings and their own bodies?

In 2003, Savana Redding was an honor student in the eighth grade with no history of disciplinary problems at Safford Middle School, which is a two-hour drive from Tucson, Arizona.

As she recounted to the *New York Times*, Savana still remembers the clothes she had on—black stretch pants with butterfly patches and a pink T-shirt—the day school officials strip-searched her.

The story begins not with Savana but with two other students.

In October 2003, a Safford Middle School student named Jordan told school administrators that certain students were bringing drugs and weapons onto campus. He also reported that he had been sick after taking some pills that "he got from a classmate" and later handed Assistant Principal Kerry Wilson a white pill (ibuprofen) that he said a student named Marissa had given him.

Wilson then called Marissa out of class. Marissa's teacher produced a day planner that had been near Marissa's reach and that contained various contraband items. In the presence of a female assistant, Wilson requested that Marissa turn out her pockets and open her wallet. Marissa produced a blue pill (determined to be naproxen, an anti-inflammatory drug), several white pills, and a razor blade. When Wilson asked where the blue pill came from, Marissa suggested it came from her friend. That friend, she said, was Savana Redding.

Wilson learned from staff members that Savana and Marissa were friends and were part of an "unusually rowdy group" who had attended a school dance during which alcohol and cigarettes were found in the girls' bathroom. In addition, Jordan had reported that before the dance he had been at a party at Savana's house where alcohol was served.

Wilson then went looking for thirteen-year-old Savana Redding in her math class.

"I was in class, and the vice principal came and got me out of class, and he started asking me some things, like questions about pills and some other contraband, and I told him, 'No, I don't know what that is, where it came from, and I haven't seen it,'" said Savana.

"He asked me if he could search my backpack. I told him, 'Yeah, go ahead.'" The backpack search produced nothing.

"So, he brought the secretary in, and then he asked me to follow her," she continued. "We ended up in the nurse's office, and then she asked me to take off my pants and my shirt, and when I did that I gave it to them, and I stood there in my underwear while they were searching in the seams, and shaking [my underwear], just looking for something, then I just, I looked down, I didn't want to look at their faces, and I didn't want to cry. You know, I didn't want to add the extra embarrassment onto it."

After she had stripped to her underwear, "they asked me to pull out my bra and move it from side to side," she said. "They made me open my legs and pull out my underwear."

No pills were found.

She says of the strip search: "[It] was the most humiliating experience I have ever had." According to Savana's attorney, after the search there was no apology or explanation. Savana was just told to go sit in the hallway for hours until school ended, and when her mother picked her up, Savana was "very withdrawn" and crying. When her mother called the school to complain, she said no one returned her phone calls.

In the legal dispute with the Redding family, lawyers for the school district claimed their actions were part of a decades-long struggle against student drug abuse and that the search was not excessively intrusive.

Her mother, April Redding, disagreed. "They changed my kid, and they need to understand what they took away from her." Savana did not return to school for months after the search, saying she "never wanted to see the secretary or the nurse ever again," and ended up transferring to another school.

The experience left her wary, nervous, and distrustful, and she developed bleeding stomach ulcers.

"Before it happened, I loved school, loved everything about it. You know, I had a 4.0 GPA, honor roll, and now, well, afterward I never wanted to go to school again."

THE CASE

April Redding filed suit on behalf of her daughter in federal court, arguing that the school district violated the protection guaranteed by the Fourth Amendment against unreasonable searches.

On June 25, 2009, the U.S. Supreme Court ruled 8 to 1 in favor of the Reddings, holding that under the Fourth Amendment school officials must have "reasonable suspicion of danger or of resort to underwear for hiding evidence of wrongdoing before a search can reasonably make the quantum leap from outer clothes and backpacks to exposure of intimate parts." The Court ruled that, because there was "no indication of danger to students" or "any reason to suppose that Savana was carrying pills in her underwear," the search of Savana Redding was unreasonable and violated the Fourth Amendment.

THE DECISION

The issue in this case was whether a thirteen-year-old student's Fourth Amendment right was violated when she was subjected to a search of her bra and underpants by school officials acting on *reasonable suspicion* that she had brought forbidden prescription and over-the-counter drugs to school. The Court held that because there were no reasons to suspect the existence of drugs that presented a danger to others or that were concealed in the student's underwear, the search violated the Fourth Amendment.

The Court indicated that, while there were enough facts to justify the initial search of Savana's belongings and outer clothing, the school exceeded the permissible scope of the search when it went on to do the strip search without any "distinct elements" or "specific suspicions" justifying that further, and much more intrusive, infringement of her privacy.

MAKING HISTORY

Savana Kedding at the U.S. Supreme Court.

Savana won her case in 2009, but the outcome was by no means a foregone conclusion. Some years after the *Safford* case had been decided, Justice Ruth Bader Ginsburg recalled how, during the oral argument, she had angrily tried to get the male justices to stop joking from the bench and to understand how a young girl would react to being told to pull out her panties and shake. She even told *USA Today* after the oral argument that her male colleagues didn't get what this kind of search would mean to a sensitive thirteen-year-old girl.

The experience was an eye opener for mother April. "I would like for every parent in the United States to understand the authority that we have given schools," she said. "I feel that from what I experienced . . . with my daughter that they can pretty much do whatever they like because they're acting in your behalf."

Redding feels some measure of vindication. "I am excited that [the Court] agreed with me, they see that it was wrong for the school to do that."

"What they did was wrong, and they feel like they didn't do anything wrong, and that really hurts, but it's more about other kids." She said the long legal battle "was to make sure it didn't happen to anyone else."

Important Concepts
Reasonableness Grounds/Reasonable Suspicion

The Fourth Amendment to the U.S. Constitution guarantees the "right of the people to be secure in their persons . . . against unreasonable searches and seizures." In most situations involving law enforcement and adults, the Supreme Court has held that the government must have *probable cause*—that is, trustworthy information sufficient to warrant a reasonable belief that the subject of a search has committed an offense and a fair probability that the search will produce evidence of wrongdoing—prior to conducting a search.

But the Supreme Court held in 1985 in the *New Jersey v. T.L.O.* case that K–12 public school officials do *not* need to have probable cause to believe that the subject of the search has violated the law. Instead, the search of a student depends on the *reasonableness* of the search—a lower standard of justification.

So, what makes a search reasonable?

First, the search must be "justified at its inception" due to the presence of "*reasonable grounds* for suspecting that the search will turn up evidence that the student has violated or is violating either the law or rules of the school." That means a school official must have a *reasonable suspicion* that there is a moderate chance of finding that a student did something wrong. (And if this sounds not far from "probable cause" to you, you are not alone; perhaps it helps to think of the difference between a solid *possibility* versus a *probability* of finding evidence of wrongdoing.)

Second, in public schools, the search actually conducted must be "*reasonably related in scope* to the circumstances that justified the interference in the first place"—which is to say, the particular method and contours of the search must be "reasonably related to the objectives of the search and not excessively intrusive in light of the age and sex of the student and the nature of the infraction."

In the *Safford* case, the Court held that the school's initial search of Savana's backpack and outer clothing was reasonable, but that's where the legality ended. The school then went way overboard with

IN FACT

The *Safford* case was decided twenty-four years after the landmark *New Jersey v. T.L.O.* case, in which the U.S. Supreme Court held that search of a student's belongings must be supported by only reasonable suspicion, as opposed to probable cause. That case involved a search of a student's purse for cigarettes and then for marijuana. Student drug use is often the focal point in these searches. In 1995 and 2002, the Supreme Court held in the *Vernonia* and *Earls* cases that random drug testing of high school athletes and drug testing of students participating in other extracurricular activities did not violate the Fourth Amendment. Protecting students from weapons is another common purpose of student searches; note that courts have generally upheld the use of walk-through and hand-held metal detectors in schools (although the use of such equipment can be costly, ineffective, detrimental to school climate, and unlawful if their use is not justified or is imposed selectively on particular students).

Notably, as of 2018, while student drug use (other than marijuana) is at its lowest levels in over two decades, K–12 school shooting incidents and deaths are at their highest levels in history; in 2018, there were nearly one hundred K–12 school shooting incidents in the United States—more than 50 percent higher than in any other previously recorded year.

an intrusive and degrading strip search that was (a) not justified by a reasonable suspicion she was carrying painkillers in her underwear and (b) beyond the scope of what was reasonable given that the school was essentially looking for pain relievers equivalent to "two Advil, or one Aleve" pill.

IMPLICATIONS FOR EDUCATORS AND SCHOOLS

- Educators have a tough job of ensuring the safety and health of students while not infringing upon their right of privacy. The *Safford* decision can be seen as making that job more challenging. But it also supports health and safety by safeguarding against searches that are so intrusive that they result in lifelong health consequences for students or irreversibly damage the relationship and trust between students and faculty. And the case reaffirms that schools do not need probable cause to search students' belongings or outer garments—only a reasonable suspicion that the student to be searched has violated school policy.

- As the *Safford* case explains, students have a reasonable expectation of privacy. A search has got to be justified from the beginning, and as it continues and becomes more intrusive, additional justification is necessary. Thus, proper training to conduct searches is essential.

Reflection

To what extent do you believe a student has a reasonable expectation of privacy over his or her belongings or body at school? Do you feel differently depending on whether the search involves undergarments, jacket or pants pockets, purses, backpacks, or lockers? Does the age or gender of the student matter? Does it matter whether the school is one that has a history of violence or where weapons or drugs are routinely discovered? Or whether the school is equipped with metal detectors, similar to airports?

GETTING PROACTIVE

- Most public schools designate responsibility for searching students to a limited number of personnel and school administrators. If you are not one of them, who are these individuals in your school? What procedures are you supposed to follow when an incident involving a possible search arises?

- A student's possession of drugs, unprescribed medications, or weapons at school is a major sign that the student is at risk (or in the middle of) a health or safety crisis. Addressing students' social, emotional, or health needs or connecting them with a school counselor or social worker (if available) may prevent future disciplinary incidents. Schools should have a school climate plan that cultivates social and emotional health among students, connects students and families with community resources, and provides individual counseling for troubled students.

- Like most of the topics raised by Supreme Court cases in this book, student privacy can and should be taught in schools. Do your students know the various types of privacy (e.g., privacy over their own bodies, privacy over sensitive medical or personal information)? Do they know how to protect their own privacy and how to respect the privacy of others? Who is responsible for teaching these concepts at your school?

- In this increasingly digital age, all educators can help ensure school-sponsored educational technology or devices do not disclose student data or information to third parties and that students understand basic digital privacy concepts and security measures and avoid sharing sensitive personal information about themselves or others online.

Classroom AND Community VOICES

High School Teacher
Rhode Island

I had a student some years ago who we suspected was using and/or selling drugs in school. I went to discuss the matter with my principal. We decided that, rather than search the student's bags and his locker, we were going to have his mother come into school in order to have a conversation with us and the school's social worker about our concerns. We reasoned that, while a search of his bag or locker might turn up proof of his drug possession, it could also damage our relationship with him and the larger culture of trust within our school. A meeting with his mother had other risks, of course, but we felt that it was a risk worth taking.

When his mother arrived at school, the five of us sat down to talk. We shared our suspicions and concerns. At first, the young man was defensive and angry, but over time (and with the help of his mother) we were able to help him understand that we were concerned about his well-being and his future.

We never did search his bags or his locker that day (or any day since). He left that afternoon with his mother, and we all signed a behavioral contract to ensure we were aligned. We agreed on a few things:

- The young man would meet regularly with the social worker to check in on how he was feeling.
- If we had reasonable suspicions of drug use or drug dealing in school, we would search his person, belongings, and locker (his mother gave us her blessing).

- If we found drugs on his person, in his bag, or in his locker, we would inform the police and his mother.
- The school would follow through with appropriate disciplinary actions (suspension and/or expulsion).

After that conversation, we never had reason to believe that the young man was using or selling drugs at school. His involvement in school improved, as did his performance, and he began to take on leadership roles.

RECENT DEVELOPMENTS

Two relatively recent cases (2016) show that the *Safford* case did not eliminate the ability of schools to conduct searches of students—even those that are intrusive in nature.

- In *D.H. by Dawson v. Clayton County School District*, the court held that the decision to conduct a strip search of a male student did not violate the Fourth Amendment because, unlike *Safford*, the school official suspected that the student possessed an illegal controlled substance and also had knowledge that on the same day another student had hidden marijuana in the waistband of his underpants. (The court also held, however, that requiring the student to fully remove his underwear in the presence of his peers was unnecessarily intrusive and excessive in scope.)

- In *A.M. v. Holmes*, the court approved a search of a student where, prior to the search, the school official found $200 in cash, a belt with a marijuana symbol, and a bandanna in the student's possession, and where the search itself only involved a partial removal of clothing (the student was not forced to take off his undershirt, underwear, and athletic shorts).

Online privacy is a quickly developing area of which educators must be aware. As recently as 2015, in *Jackson v. Ladner*, a federal court concluded that the law was not settled in 2007 (when the incident in question took place) that school officials could not, consistent with the Fourth Amendment, access a student's social-networking account after receiving information that the student had sent threatening online messages to another student. The student-plaintiff had alleged that her constitutional right to privacy was violated when the school official obtained her Facebook log-in information, searched her account, and then disseminated the content of her messages to other school officials. In the last several years, however, the Supreme Court has acted to limit the government's access to individuals' digital information, given the extraordinary amount of personal information contained online and on personal smartphones. Therefore, arguably, schools should exercise caution when conducting searches of students' online social-networking information, as it is increasingly clear such actions implicate the Fourth Amendment.

GETTING MORE INFORMATION

Here's a list of national-level organizations that provide more in-depth information or further resources on the Fourth Amendment, student privacy, and student health and safety. This list is not exhaustive. You may also wish to look up state and local resources, including resources offered by your own school district. This is particularly important in this area as state and local laws and policies vary greatly in search policies and procedures (see, for example, California Education Code Section 49050: "No school employee shall conduct a search that involves: (a) Conducting a body cavity search of a pupil manually or with an instrument; (b) Removing or arranging any or all of the clothing of a pupil to permit a visual inspection of the underclothing, breast, buttocks, or genitalia of the pupil"; see also New York City Department of Education Regulation of the Chancellor No. A-432 (Issued 9/13/05): "Under no circumstance shall a strip-search of a student be conducted").

- Electronic Frontier Foundation, https://www.eff.org (see "student privacy")

- National Center on Safe and Supportive Learning Environments (see state by state laws re: "use of student and locker searches"), https://safesupportivelearning.ed.gov

- Substance Abuse and Mental Health Services Administration, https://www.samhsa.gov (see "Safe Schools/Healthy Students Success Stories")

- U.S. Department of Education, https://studentprivacy.ed.gov (see "for K–12 school officials")

CASE 10

Goss v. Lopez (1975)

Students facing discipline have a right of due process.

As educators, you know the importance of keeping students focused in the classroom. You also know that appropriately responding to students who disrupt the learning environment is key to teaching and learning.

At the same time, student discipline practices are under scrutiny as never before; nationwide data shows that certain students—especially black students and students with disabilities—are suspended at two to four times the rate of white students and students without disabilities. Students of color are also arrested at school and are subject to referrals to law enforcement at higher rates than other children—a phenomenon that often originates with disciplinary incidents and has contributed to a "school-to-prison" pipeline.

Although most incidents involving discipline stop short of suspension or expulsion from school, some do not. What rights do students have in these situations? What are the emerging legal and policy developments around discipline in K–12 schools? This chapter explores these questions, using *Goss v. Lopez* as a starting point.

In the spring of 1971, during a period of heightened racial consciousness, several schools in the Columbus, Ohio, public schools were affected by race-related confrontations, demonstrations, and other examples of student activism.

Dwight Lopez was a nineteen-year-old student at Central High School in Columbus. Tension had mounted at Central High School during Black History Week. On the morning of February 26, 1971, while Dwight was in the lunchroom, students came in and started overturning tables. Dwight claimed that he took no part in the unlawful activity and that he did not violate any school rules and instead walked out of the scene and went home. However, later that day he was notified by the principal that he had been suspended from school. He was not told why. But his parents received a letter from the principal stating that Dwight was in a group of students who had disrupted the school program—and that he was to stay at home until further notice.

A school meeting regarding Dwight's discipline was set for March 8—two weeks after the lunchroom incident. On March 8, Dwight went with his mother and a sister to the disciplinary meeting, but the entrance of the building was blocked by several hundred persons protesting board of education policies. Dwight and his family attempted to follow up with district officials but received no response; no hearing ever took place.

Weeks later, on March 24, 1971, Dwight was transferred from Central High School to the Adult Day School. He did not request this transfer and did not attend the Adult Day School; however, he went to the Adult Night School and received his diploma on June 10, 1972.

THE CASE

Dwight was not alone in his suspension. He later testified that at least seventy-five other students had been suspended from his school. He eventually joined in a lawsuit with eight other students who had attended other schools in the district, arguing that by issuing blanket suspensions to all identifiable students at a given time or place, the school district had swept in innocent victims who had merely been in the wrong place at the wrong time.

The students also argued that no hearing or conference designed to elicit the truth was conducted; that their suspensions led to longer-term separations from school, the loss of substantial credits required for graduation, and permanent negative entries in their school records; and that they suffered from a loss of self-esteem, feelings of withdrawal and helplessness, and stigma from being labeled as deviant or a troublemaker by school officials and teachers, family, and friends.

On January 22, 1975, the U.S. Supreme Court invalidated the suspensions of Dwight and other students, holding that, under the Due Process Clause of the U.S. Constitution, students who are facing a temporary suspension of ten days or less must be given oral or written notice of what they've done, an explanation of the evidence the school has, and a chance to tell their side of the story.

THE DECISION

The Court ruled in favor of the suspended students, holding that students' public education "may not be taken away for misconduct without adherence to the minimum procedures required by [the Due Process] Clause."

Those minimum procedures include "some kind of notice" and "some kind of hearing," the Court stated. In other words, "the student must be given oral or written notice of the charges against him and, if he denies them, an explanation of the evidence the authorities have and an opportunity to present his side of the story."

Importantly, this case outlined basic due process involving suspensions not exceeding ten days. "Longer suspensions or expulsions for the remainder of the school term, or permanently, may require more formal procedures," the Court stated. (More on this later.)

MAKING HISTORY

Attorney Peter Roos believes that the *Goss* case established a baseline protection for students against arbitrary discipline.

Peter Roos was a staff attorney at the Center for Law and Education at Harvard University when the case involving Dwight Lopez and other students suspended from school in Columbus, Ohio, was referred to him. (Roos, who graduated from Occidental College in 1964 and Hastings College of Law in 1967, eventually left Harvard to become the education litigation director at the Mexican American Legal Defense and Education Fund (MALDEF). At MALDEF, he went on to litigate another famous case in this book: *Plyler v. Doe*.)

In 1985, ten years removed from the *Goss* ruling, Roos said, "Teachers and principals are much more likely to be concerned about documentation when a suspension or expulsion is involved than they were before *Goss* . . . I think it's fair to assume that much,

continues

though not all, of the arbitrariness has been eliminated from the suspension process."

Today many would consider Roos' assumption premature, as federal data continue to show that students of color—like those Roos represented in *Goss v. Lopez*—are suspended and expelled from school in far greater proportions than their white peers.

But Roos believes that the *Goss* case moved the country forward in subtle yet important ways. "It was important to establish some minimal protection for short-term suspension . . . as a foundation on which to build greater protections when the harms were greater."

He believes the case encouraged more educators to find better ways to address student behavior problems. "I believe that *Goss* has contributed to the development of alternatives to suspension, such as the 'cooling off' room," he said. "Though some of these alternatives have problems of their own, I cannot but see them as an improvement over total exclusion from school."

Important Concepts

Two pillars of due process include the rights to adequate *notice* and a *hearing*. Other rights are often associated with those rights, such as the rights to counsel or to cross-examine witnesses. But what kind of notice or hearing is required before suspending a K–12 student for ten days or less? Even after the *Goss* case, the answer is: very little.

Notice

The Court very simply held that a school must tell students why they are being suspended *before* the school suspends them. If this doesn't sound like much notice at all, that's because that is what the Court intended. In fact, the Court stated, "[i]n the great majority of cases the disciplinarian may informally discuss the alleged misconduct with the student minutes after it has occurred" and "there need be no delay between the time notice is given and the time of the hearing."

IN FACT

The suspension of the students in the *Goss* case did not occur in a vacuum. In July 1969, riots and fire bombings were sparked by the killing of a black father by a white dry cleaner on Columbus' Near East Side. In January 1970, the murder of a black man by a white police officer known as "Machine Gun Morgan" sparked racial tension that only escalated upon the officer's acquittal in March 1971.

College campuses in Ohio and nationwide were hotbeds of protest in the early 1970s. In May 1970, National Guardsmen shot and killed four students at Ohio's Kent State University during Vietnam-era protests. Days earlier, the Guardsmen also tear-gassed thousands of students at Ohio State University in Columbus, Ohio; hundreds of students were arrested and dozens hospitalized, including several from gunshot wounds. During this period, some estimate that half the country's student population were taking part in anti-war activities.

Columbus' public schools were also rocked between 1969 and 1971, when, after years of unmet demands and frustration with continued segregation and inequality in the city's school system, the city's high schools were the scene of boycotts, sit-ins, protests and, in the case of Central High—the school that Dwight Lopez, who was involved in the *Goss* case, attended—the shooting of two black youths by a white student. By early 1971, when the students in *Goss* were suspended, several of the system's schools were "nearly out of control," with reports of attempted fire bombings at one school and racial tensions temporarily shutting down Central High and another school. The attempt by black students at Linden-McKinley High to replace an American flag with a black nationalism flag at school led to the school's closure and the stationing of more than fifty Columbus police officers around the building.

"We hold only that, in being given an opportunity to explain his version of the facts at [an informal hearing or discussion], the student first be told what he is accused of doing and what the basis of the accusation is."

The Court even stated that the notice (and hearing) requirement could be dispensed with altogether until after a student's suspension (although they should occur as soon as practicable) if the student posed a "continuing danger to persons or property or an ongoing threat of disrupting the academic process."

Of course, most schools have detailed procedures providing for greater and more formal notice to students (and their parents) than what the Court outlined in *Goss*—even for short suspensions. But that extra notice is, in the vast majority of cases, not required by federal law.

Hearing Process

Similarly, in articulating the *hearing* requirement, the Court was not contemplating anything fancy here. "At least an informal give-and-take between student and disciplinarian" is required, and no more. The Court explicitly stopped short of requiring, for short suspensions, that students be given the opportunity to obtain a lawyer, to confront and cross-examine witnesses, or to call their own witnesses to verify their own version of an incident. Why? Because the Court wished to avoid turning schools into mini-courtrooms for all types of disciplinary actions, which could "overwhelm" schools and "cost more than it would save in educational effectiveness."

As with the notice requirement, schools can and do regularly exceed what *Goss* required for disciplinary hearings. Most schools schedule more formal conferences or meetings even for short-term suspensions rather than simply having an informal conversation with the student they seek to suspend.

IMPLICATIONS FOR EDUCATORS AND SCHOOLS

- It is important to know that the *Goss* case does *not* mean that educators and schools cannot discipline students or remove them from school when necessary. This is a case about appropriate disciplinary *processes*, not the use of discipline per se.

- At the same time, the case serves as a reminder that even short-term interruptions in learning are serious; therefore, suspensions must be accompanied by adherence to proper procedures, especially with respect to the notice and informal hearing requirements.

- The Every Student Succeeds Act (ESSA) (which replaced No Child Left Behind) requires states and school districts to describe annually in state and local report cards how they will support efforts to improve school conditions for student learning through reducing the overuse of discipline. They must also publish and report annually the rates of suspensions and expulsions in their schools. States also have discretion under ESSA to include school climate and safety (which could include addressing student discipline) as major components of their statewide accountability system.

- The students who were disciplined in the *Goss* case included students of color who were living in a time of great racial tension and unrest in their schools and communities. The disproportionate discipline of students of color and students with disabilities remains a serious civil rights issue today; schools who discipline students in different ways or at different rates depending on their race or disability status risk inviting a civil rights investigation or lawsuit.

- *Goss* covers federal due process requirements for public schools; the existence of such requirements for private schools, if any, must arise out of state or local laws or customs.

Reflection

Consider the following statistics and reflect upon incidents of discipline in your classroom, school, or district. Which of the statistics below surprises you? Which come as no surprise?

Teachers report widespread concerns around student discipline:

- About 80 percent of Oklahoma City teachers who responded to a union survey said they are responsible for administering the majority of student discipline, while nearly half said they have a student with a chronic discipline problem who should not be in their classroom.

- Sixty-two percent of New York teachers who responded to a different survey indicated their schools do not have sufficient staff to provide intervention services to help students who act out; more than 80 percent of the respondents said students in their schools lost learning time as a result of other disruptive students.

Disparities in who receives discipline are widespread. According to federal data:

- About 2.7 million (between 5 and 6 percent) of all K–12 students in the United States received one or more out-of-school suspensions during the 2015–16 school year.

- Black male students represented 8 percent of enrolled students and accounted for 25 percent of students who received an out-of-school suspension.

- Black female students represented 8 percent of the student enrollment and accounted for 14 percent of students who received an out-of-school suspension.

- Students with disabilities represented 12 percent of students enrolled and 26 percent of students who received an out-of-school suspension.

- Black students (male and female) represented 15 percent of the total student enrollment, and 31 percent of students who were referred to law enforcement or subject to a school-related arrest.

GETTING PROACTIVE

- If you work or teach at a public school, look up the civil rights data on student discipline for your (a) school and (b) district: https://ocrdata.ed.gov. Does the data seem accurate to you? Do you notice disparities in discipline for students of different racial backgrounds? For students with disabilities? Consider using the data as a discussion point at a future staff meeting, or examine the data with students.

- Most times, the response to student behavior is not a legal issue but a pedagogical one. See Getting More Information for some resources that can help educators and schools prevent student behavioral issues from escalating or resulting in suspension or expulsion.

Classroom AND Community VOICES

High School Principal
Rhode Island

For some time, we struggled to figure out how to reintegrate students who had been in an in-school fight. (To be clear, the fights I'm referring to did not involve bullying or harassment. We treated those cases differently.) Meeting with the parents and suspending both students to let them "cool off" did not seem to accomplish our goals. So, we tried something different. We worked together as a staff to test-pilot a new process.

When two students had a fight in school, we'd separate them and work with each student to calm them down and make sure both parties were safe. We would call the parents, share what happened, and explain our process moving forward. The goal was always to reintegrate both students back into the school.

- First, the parent or guardian would come to school to pick up the child. We'd meet with the guardian and child to review the events and discuss next steps and make a plan to reintegrate the student back into school.

- Next (usually the following day), we'd conduct a mediation between both parties.

- After the mediation, both students would publicly apologize to the whole school community (we had short whole-school meetings three times per week). During that meeting, each student would explain how he/she/they would "make repair" to the school community. We'd decide on the repair mechanism with the student's family. Usually the repair mechanism was a small service project or a letter of reflection about the importance of community.

- Once the students apologized (usually the day after the fight took place), they would rejoin the school community and complete their project within the week.

After we instituted this process (and built the peer-mediation program) the number of fights in our school dropped over time. Now, the vast majority of our arguments/disagreements are resolved by peer mediators before a fight even begins. We're happy with our process because it helps kids learn to manage their emotions, talk things out, and make the crucial transition into adulthood.

Alex Corbitt
Middle School English Teacher, New York

Many educators think of student behavior and disciplinary procedures as an inevitable byproduct of working in a school environment, without understanding their own influence on—or even their contribution to—classroom disruptions and the widespread system of pushing certain students out of school through suspension, expulsion, and eventual entanglement with the criminal justice system: the *school-to-prison pipeline*. I was one of those educators.

I taught seventh-grade language arts at a public middle school in the Bronx, New York. Our student population was predominantly black and Latinx. During my first two years of teaching, I struggled to foster a healthy classroom environment. I prioritized discipline and management over community building and culturally sustaining pedagogy. I spent more time policing students than giving them opportunities to flourish. This was particularly problematic given that I am a white teacher working with children of color.

Over time, I realized that what and how I teach has a direct impact on my classroom environment. And so I decided to shift my pedagogical approach to teaching. I learned to listen to students and align my curricula with their needs and identities. As a class, we began to read culturally diverse texts, engage in community projects, and collaborate on projects with family members. When tensions manifested in my classroom, instead of treating them as discipline issues unrelated to my teaching, I facilitated restorative conversations with students and determined how the classroom space could better meet students' needs to reduce those tensions.

I've realized that schools are often sites of oppression and cultural assimilation or dislocation, especially for students of color. Educators are often complicit in this systemic problem. It is irresponsible for educators to resort only to discipline and suspension when students experience trauma and frustration. We also need proactive policies, curricula, and pedagogy that emphasize students' right to a humane, emotionally supportive, and culturally sustaining education.

RECENT DEVELOPMENTS

A sample of recent cases confirms that while *Goss v. Lopez* certainly established a minimal baseline due process protection for students, other courts have not, in subsequent years, extended that protection much further. In fact, in general, courts have been careful to limit *Goss* in ways that provide schools with a great deal of flexibility and few legal requirements in disciplinary situations.

- A student's transfer to an alternative education program does not constitute a harm that raises due process concerns. *Harris ex rel. Harris v. Pontotoc Cty. Sch. Dist.*, 635 F.3d 685, 690 (5th Cir. 2011).

- Students are not required to receive written notice of their suspension, nor are they entitled to cross-examine an anonymous student informant and be told that student's identity. *Heyne v. Metro. Nashville Pub. Sch.*, 655 F.3d 556, 565 (6th Cir. 2011).

- Due process is not necessarily violated when the school official who initiates or investigates charges against a student plays a role in the decision to suspend the student. *Heyne v. Metro. Nashville Pub. Sch.*, 655 F.3d 556, 569 (6th Cir. 2011).

- A one-day in-school suspension does not implicate due process requirements. *Laney v. Farley*, 501 F.3d 577, 584 (6th Cir. 2007).

- A student faced with expulsion has the right to a hearing in front of an impartial decision-maker but not a full-blown, court-like process; similarly, a student faced with a suspension longer than ten days must be afforded an informal hearing and an opportunity to defend himself, but not much more beyond that. See *Jahn v. Farnsworth*, 617 F. App'x 453, 461 (6th Cir. 2015) (citing other cases).

GETTING MORE INFORMATION

Here's a list of national-level organizations that provide more in-depth information or resources on student discipline. As you are probably aware, the control over discipline in public schools is largely controlled at the school-district level; state law runs a distant second in this arena, although many states significantly limit suspensions in schools, especially for elementary school students. In recent years, the federal government has provided civil rights guidance and other supportive resources for schools on student discipline. But in this area, you'll want to turn to your own school or district's policies and procedures as a first step.

- Education Commission of the States, www.ecs.org (see "50-State Comparison: State Policies on School Discipline")

- National Center on Safe Supportive Learning Environments, https://safesupportivelearning.ed.gov

- Supportive School Discipline Communities of Practice, https://ssdcop.neglected-delinquent.ed.gov

- Technical Assistance Center for Positive Behavioral Interventions and Supports, https://www.pbis.org

- U.S. Department of Education, www.ed.gov (see "School Climate and Discipline")

Endnotes

Chapter 1

Pages 2–3: these excerpted and paraphrased facts from the *Davis* case—and all judicial opinions or cases referenced in this book—may be found at https://www.law.cornell.edu (search under "Primary Sources: Supreme Court" for U.S. Supreme Court cases); the legal citation here is *Davis v. Monroe County Board of Education*, 119 S.Ct. 1661 (1999).

Page 3: *the federal law known as Title IX states* . . . the legal citation for Title IX, a federal statute, is 20 U.S.C. Section 1681(a); you may find all statutes referenced in this book at https://www.law.cornell.edu (search under "Primary Sources: U.S. Code" for federal, i.e., "United States Code," statutes).

Page 4: *Making History* section . . . see Verna Williams, "My Supreme Court Debut: Flattered, Excited and Obligated," *Portfolio Media, Inc.*, Oct. 4, 2017, https://www.law360.com.

Page 5: *In Fact* section . . . see "2015–2016 Civil Rights Data Collection: School Climate and Safety Data Highlights," U.S. Dep't of Educ. Office for Civil Rights, Apr. 2018, https://www.ed.gov.

Page 6: *constellation of surrounding circumstances* . . . *children may regularly interact* . . . see *Davis*, 119 S.Ct. at 1665.

Page 12: *Students who are subjected to homophobic epithets* . . . see "Dear Colleague Letter," U.S. Dep't of Educ. Office for Civil Rights, Oct. 26, 2010; "OCR-DOJ Letter to Richard Tehachapi Unified School District," U.S. Dep't of Educ. Office for Civil Rights (OCR Case No. 09-11-1031, DOJ Case No. DJ 169-11E-38), June 29, 2011, https://www.ed.gov.

Page 12: *Recent Developments* section . . . *The ubiquity of the Internet* . . . see Kevin Welner, Robert Kim, and Stuart Biegel, *Legal Issues in Education: Rights and Responsibilities in U.S. Public Schools Today* (St. Paul, MN: West Academic Publishing, 2017), 100–101.

Chapter 2

Pages 14–16: Introduction and *Making History* section generally . . . see Catherine Winter, "A Supreme Court Case 35 Years Ago Yields a Supply of Emboldened DACA Students Today," *APM Reports*, American Public Media Group, Aug. 21, 2017.

Pages 14–15: *The Case* section generally, including reference to the U.S. Constitution . . . see the U.S. Supreme Court opinion in the *Plyler* case . . . see *Plyler v. Doe*, 102 S.Ct. 1282 (1982), 2389–92, 2401–02.

Pages 17–18: *The Decision* section . . . see *Plyler*, 102 S.Ct. at 2394, 2396–97, 2399.

Pages 18–19: *Important Concepts* section . . . *The Equal Protection Clause* . . . see U.S. Constitution, Amendment XIV, at https://www.law.cornell.edu (search under "Primary Sources: Constitution").

Pages 19–20: *Important Concepts* section . . . *rational basis* discussion . . . see *Plyler*, 102 S.Ct. at 2400–02.

Page 19: *In Fact* section . . . see R. Capps, M. Fix, and J. Zong, "A Profile of U.S. Children with Unauthorized Immigrant Parents," Migration Policy Institute, Jan. 2016, https://www.migrationpolicy.org.

Page 21: *Implications section . . .* see "Guidance for School Districts to Ensure Equal Access for All Children to Public Schools, Regardless of Immigration Status," May 8, 2014, U.S. Dep't of Educ. Office for Civil Rights, https://www.ed.gov.

Pages 21–22: *Immigration-related enforcement actions (including "raids") . . .* see "FAQ on Sensitive Locations and Courthouse Arrests," U.S. Immigrations and Customs Enforcement, https://www.ice.gov.

Page 22: *massive attendance drop-offs and increased student anxiety and health problems . . .* see Melinda Anderson, "How Fears of Deportation Harm Kids' Education," *The Atlantic*, May 26, 2016.

Pages 22–23: *Getting Proactive section . . .* see "Top 10 Ways to Support Undocumented Students," Immigrants Rising, https://immigrantsrising.org.

Page 24: *In a recent UCLA survey . . .* Patricia Gándara and Jongyeon Ee, "U.S. Immigration Enforcement Policy and its Impact on Teaching and Learning in the Nation's Schools," UCLA Civil Rights Project, Feb. 28, 2018, https://www.civilrightsproject .ucla.edu.

Page 24: *Educators themselves have experienced additional stress . . .* see S. Sanchez, R. Freeman, and P. Martin, "Stressed, Overworked, and Not Sure Whom to Trust: How Public School Educators are Navigating Recent Immigration Enforcement," UCLA Civil Rights Project, Feb. 28, 2018, https://www.civilrightsproject.ucla.edu.

Page 24: *"One of my students let me know that she was going to court with her parents the next day" . . .* Written response from Julie Jee, December 18, 2018.

Page 24: *The Trump administration also announced in 2017 that it intended to end the Deferred Action for Childhood Arrivals (DACA) program . . .* see David Nakamura, "Trump Administration Announces End of Immigration Protection Program for 'Dreamers,'" *Washington Post*, Sept. 5, 2017.

Page 24: *Congress has yet to pass what is known as the DREAM Act . . .* see Rafael Bernal, "House Dems Reintroduce the Dream Act," *The Hill*, Mar. 12, 2019.

Chapter 3

Pages 26–27: *by the late 1980s the segregation of black and white students in the South had reached a low point . . . today, all of the desegregation gains in the South achieved since 1967 have been wiped out, and schools throughout the nation remain deeply segregated by race . . .* see G. Orfield et al., "Brown at 60: Great Progress, a Long Retreat and an Uncertain Future," UCLA Civil Rights Project, May 2014, https://www.civilrightsproject.ucla.edu.

Page 27: *And in recent decades, parents . . . have filed lawsuits . . .* see *Parents Involved in Community Schools v. Seattle School District No. 1*, 551 U.S. 701 (2007), 724 (citing recent lawsuits challenging race-conscious school assignment plans).

Page 27: *Kathleen Brose — a PTA member, volunteer music teacher, and mother of two . . . Ballard High, nestled on a thirteen-acre campus . . . But Elisabeth ended up at her fourth choice . . .* see Cara Sandberg, "The Story of Parents Involved in Community Schools," Boalt Hall School of Law, accessed Apr. 17, 2019, https://www.law.berkeley.edu/our-faculty /faculty-sites/steve-sugarman/student-papers/educational-law-stories-student-papers-from/.

Pages 27–28, 30: *The Case section . . .* Many factual details come from the U.S. Supreme Court opinion itself, see *Parents Involved*, 127 S.Ct. 2738 (2007), 2746–50, 2755, 2768.

Page 29: *After learning that the Supreme Court had ruled in her favor, Kathleen Brose said . . . Today, nearly six times as many schools in Seattle are classified as intensely segregated . . .* see Ashley Gross, "Since 1990, Seattle's Schools Have Become More Segregated, Even as Neighborhoods Integrated," KNKX Radio, https://www.knkx.org, Dec. 3, 2018.

Page 29: *Sean Riley, an African American educator who is also a product of Seattle Public Schools, observes . . .* see Sean Riley, "How Seattle Gave Up on Busing and Allowed Its Public Schools to Become Alarmingly Resegregated," *The Stranger*, Apr. 13, 2016.

Pages 30–32: *The Decision* section . . . see *Parents Involved*, 127 S.Ct. at 2754, 2756–57.

Page 31: *In Fact* section generally, especially desegregation trends . . . see Gary Orfield et al., "Brown at 62: School Segregation by Race, Poverty, and State," UCLA Civil Rights Project, May 16, 2016, https://www.civilrightsproject.ucla.edu.

Pages 32–33: *Important Concepts* section . . . see *Parents Involved*, 127 S.Ct. at 2760, 2792.

Page 36: *in 2014, for the first time, nationwide, more than 50 percent of the school-age population was nonwhite . . .* see "State Nonfiscal Survey of Public Elementary and Secondary Education, 1995–96 through 2013–14"; and "National Elementary and Secondary Enrollment by Race/Ethnicity Projection Model, 1972 through 2025," Common Core of Data (CCD), U.S. Dep't of Educ. National Center for Education Statistics, https://nces.ed.gov.

Page 36: *in the state of New York, nearly two out of three black and Latinx students attend schools that are overwhelmingly (90 percent or above) black and Latinx . . .* see Orfield, G., et al., "Brown at 62," 5–6.

Page 36: *admission policies to specialized New York City high schools that exacerbate segregation are a current flashpoint in local politics there . . .* Eliza Shapiro, "Only 7 Black Students Got into N.Y.'s Most Selective High School, Out of 895 Spots," *New York Times*, Mar. 18, 2019.

Page 37: *Lower Merion School District in Pennsylvania adopted a redistricting plan that . . .* see *Doe ex rel. Doe v. Lower Merion School District*, 665 F.3d 524 (2011).

Page 37: *In 2018, the Trump Administration rescinded a U.S. Department of Education policy on the "voluntary use of race" in student assignment . . .* see Mark Walsh, "Trump Rescinds Obama-Era Guidance on Diversity at Schools," *Education Week*, July 17, 2018; and "Dear Colleague Letter" on how educational institutions can lawfully pursue voluntary policies to achieve diversity or avoid racial isolation, Dec. 2, 2011 (rescinded and archived), U.S. Dep't of Educ. Office for Civil Rights, https://www.ed.gov.

Chapter 4

Page 39: *The basic parameters of the IEP . . . were established by the Supreme Court in 1982 in the* Rowley *case . . .* see *Board of Ed. of Hendrick Hudson Central School Dist., Westchester Cty. v. Rowley*, 458 U.S. 176 (1982).

Pages 39–40, 42: Introduction generally . . . many factual details come from the *Endrew F.* case itself, see *Endrew F. v. Douglas County School District RE-1*, 137 S.Ct. 988 (2017), and from Ann Schimke, "Inside One Colorado Family's Long Legal Journey to Affirm Their Son's Right to a Meaningful Education," *Chalkbeat*, Nov. 15, 2017.

Page 41: *Making History* section . . . see Schimke, "Inside One Colorado Family's Long Legal Journey."

Page 42: *The Case* section. . . see *Endrew F.*, 137 S.Ct. at 1001.

Pages 42–43: *The Decision* section. . . see *Endrew F.*, 137 S.Ct. at 1000, 1002.

Pages 43–44: *Important Concepts* section. . . see *ibid.* at 999.

Page 44: *In Fact* section . . . *Thirteen percent (6.7 million) of all students in public schools receive special education services* . . . see "Digest of Education Statistics 2017, Table 204.30," National Center for Education Statistics, U.S. Dep't of Educ. Office of Special Education Programs, https://nces.ed.gov.

Page 44: *In Fact* section . . . *Between 2009 and 2016, the U.S. Department of Education received 36,790 disability-related civil rights complaints* . . . see "Achieving Simple Justice," U.S. Dep't of Educ. Office for Civil Rights (2016), https://www.ed.gov.

Pages 45–46: *Implications* section . . . for the Individuals with Disabilities Education Act, see 20 U.S.C. Section 1400 *et seq.*; for Section 504 of Rehabilitation Act of 1973, see 29 U.S.C. Section 794 *et seq.*; for the Americans with Disabilities Act of 1990, see 42 U.S.C. Section 12101 *et seq.*; for the Every Student Succeeds Act, see 20 U.S.C. Section 6301 *et seq.*, https://www.law.cornell.edu (search under "Primary Sources: U.S. Code" for federal, i.e., "United States Code," statutes).

Page 48: *school districts are still winning the vast majority of disability-related court cases that have been decided since mid-2017* . . . see Christina A. Samuels, "A Year Ago the Supreme Court Raised the Bar for Special Ed: What's Happened Since?," *Education Week*, Apr. 27, 2018.

Page 48: *But there are signs that schools are settling Endrew-F.–like cases in favor of the student* . . . see, for example, Ann Schimke, "Douglas County District Pays $1.3 Million to Settle Landmark Special Education case," *Chalkbeat*, June 20, 2018.

Page 49: *In recent years, there have been cases involving the right of students with disabilities to participate in team sports* . . . see *Bingham v. Oregon School Activities Ass'n*, 24 F.Supp.2d 1110 (D. Oregon 1998) . . . *to accessible school websites* . . . see Ely Frankovich, "Spokane Schools Swept Up in Nationwide Barrage of ADA Website Challenges," *Spokesman-Review*, Aug. 9, 2017 . . . *to accommodations for food allergies* . . . see *T.F. v. Fox Chapel Area School District*, 589 Fed.Appx. 594 (3d Cir. 2014).

Chapter 5

Pages 50–51: *the U.S. Supreme Court has, over the years, determined that we have a fundamental right to educate our own children as we see fit—for example, to homeschool them for religious reasons or send them to private school* . . . see *Wisconsin v. Yoder*, 406 U.S. 205 (1972), *Pierce v. Society of the Sisters*, 268 U.S. 510 (1925).

Page 51: Introduction . . . *Demetrio Rodriguez was born a migrant-farm-working family* . . . see Elaine Ayela, "Rodriguez, Who Fought for Equality, Dies at 87," *San Antonio Express-News*, Apr. 23, 2013.

Page 51: *Demetrio's son Alex recalls his elementary school's leaky windows* . . . *The conditions upset Demetrio* . . . *the Edgewood district could raise only $50 per student from property taxes while the wealthier Alamo Heights district could raise $500 per student* . . . see Laura Isensee, "How a Dad Helped Start the Fight for Better Public School Funding in Texas," *Houston Public Media*, Sept. 7, 2015.

Page 52: *Historically, funding for Texas public schools was structured such that 10 percent came from the federal government* . . . see C. Ogletree and K. Robinson, *The Enduring Legacy of Rodriguez* (Cambridge, MA: Harvard Education Press, 2015), 4.

Page 52: *The Case* section generally . . . most facts come from the U.S. Supreme Court opinion itself, see *San Antonio Independent School District v. Rodriguez,* 93 S.Ct. 1278 (1973), 1282, 1285–86.

Page 52: *Demetrio Rodriguez helped to form an association of Mexican American parents* . . . see Ogletree and Robinson, *The Enduring Legacy of Rodriguez,* 3.

Page 53: *Making History* section . . . *Demetrio persisted, eventually securing a victory on behalf of Edgewood district students in Texas state court in 1984* . . . see Isensee, "How a Dad Helped Start the Fight."

Page 53: *"He wasn't just thinking about me and my brothers at that time. He was thinking about . . . future kids"* . . . see *ibid.*

Page 53: *"He was my hero," said daughter Patricia (and subsequent quotes)* . . . see Ayela, "Rodriguez, Who Fought for Equality, Dies at 87."

Pages 53–55: *The Decision* section generally . . . see *Rodriguez,* 93 S.Ct. at 1287–88, 1291.

Page 54: *In Fact* section . . . see Bruce Baker et al., "Is School Funding Fair?: A National Report Card, 7th ed.," Rutgers University and the Education Law Center, Feb. 2018.

Page 55: *the Supreme Court largely sidestepped the issue of race in its opinion* . . . see *ibid.* at 1288–89.

Pages 55–56: *In the end, threw up its hands and concluded* . . . see *ibid.* at 1294.

Page 56: *With this argument, the Court spied a slippery slope* . . . see *ibid.* at 1299.

Page 56: *"Nothing this Court holds today in any way detracts from our historic dedication to public education"* . . . see *ibid.* at 1295.

Page 57: *in 2014–2015, the percentages of total school revenues coming from federal, state, and local sources in Illinois . . . And in Illinois, local property taxes provided 59 percent of all school funds, whereas in Vermont that figure was* zero *percent* . . . see "National Public Education Financial Survey, 2014–15," U.S. Dep't of Educ., National Center for Education Statistics, Common Core of Data (CCD).

Page 57: *In the landmark case, Brown v. Board of Education, the Supreme Court, in outlawing racial segregation in schools, recognized the importance of education to our democratic society* . . . see *Brown v. Bd. of Educ.,* 74 S.Ct. 686 (1954).

Page 59: *Research shows that teachers spend on average $500 a year on school supplies* . . . see Moriah Balingit, "Teachers Shelling Out Nearly $500 a Year on School Supplies, Report Finds," *Washington Post,* May 15, 2018.

Pages 60–61: *Many state constitutions have provisions establishing a duty of the state to provide for public education* . . . see Emily Parker, "Fifty-State Review: Constitutional Obligations for Public Education." Education Commission of the States, Mar. 2016, https://www.ecs.org.

Page 61: *In recent years, several state courts (for example, Kansas and New Mexico) have concluded that the system of school finance violates the state's constitution; but others (for example, Connecticut and Texas) have held the opposite* . . . see Center for Educational Equity at Teachers College, http://schoolfunding.info.

Page 61: *Although the federal judge in the case agreed that literacy is vitally important to public life—and that the conditions in Detroit public schools are "devastating"* . . . Lorelei Laird, "Judge Dismisses Lawsuit Alleging Constitutional Right to Literacy; Plaintiffs Vow Appeal," *ABA Journal,* July 3, 2018.

Chapter 6

Page 64: *In 1969, when Kinney was five, he and his mother moved to San Francisco, where they were later joined by his father, a carpenter* . . . Charlie Euchner, "Languages, Law and San Francisco," *Education Week*, Jan. 25, 1984.

Page 64: *California law stated that "English shall be the basic language of instruction in all schools"*. . . see *Lau v. Nichols*, 94 S.Ct. 786 (1974), 788.

Page 64: *Edward Steinman was an advocate working in the Chinatown office of the San Francisco Neighborhood Legal Assistance Foundation in the late 1960s* . . . see Garance Burke, "Ambivalent in Any Language," *Boston Globe*, Jul. 22, 2002.

Pages 65–66: *Making History* section . . . *Kinney Lau . . . is apparently a "reluctant poster child" for bilingual education . . . "If you throw [EL students] in the classroom and tell them to sink or swim, there's a much bigger probability that they're going to sink" . . . "The thing about America is that if you're not native Indian, then you're an immigrant by default"* . . . see Burke, "Ambivalent in Any Language."

Page 66: *The Case* section . . . see *Lau*, 94 S.Ct. at 789.

Page 67: *Title VI of the Civil Rights Act of 1964 prohibits discrimination based on race, color, or national origin* . . . See 42 U.S.C. Section 2000d-1, https://www.law.cornell.edu (search under "Primary Sources: U.S. Code" for federal, i.e., "United States Code," statutes).

Page 67: *Senator Hubert Humphrey, during the floor debates on the Civil Rights Act of 1964, famously explained* . . . see *ibid.* at 789.

Pages 67–68: *Important Concepts* section . . . see *Lau*, 94 S.Ct. at 788.

Page 68: *In the same year that the Court issued the Lau ruling, Congress enacted the Equal Educational Opportunities Act (EEOA)* . . . see 20 U.S.C. § 1703(f), https://www.law.cornell.edu (search under "Primary Sources: U.S. Code" for federal, i.e., "United States Code," statutes).

Pages 68–69: *Then, six years after Lau, a federal appellate court articulated a process to determine whether schools' EL programs comply with civil rights laws* . . . see *Castañeda v. Pickard*, 648 F.2d 989 (5th Cir. 1981).

Pages 69–70: *In 2015, the U.S. Departments of Education and Justice articulated ten specific items . . . for schools to focus on to ensure equality for EL students* . . . see "Dear Colleague Letter: English Learner Students and Limited English Proficient Parents," U.S. Departments of Education and Justice, Jan. 7, 2015, https://www.ed.gov.

Page 70: *In Fact* section . . . see "Local Education Agency Universe Survey, 2015–16," U.S. Dep't of Educ. National Center for Education Statistics, Common Core of Data (CCD).

Page 71: *Consider this 2007 reflection by attorney Edward Steinman in the Lau case* . . . see Mary Ann Zehr, "Examining the Impact of *Lau v. Nichols*," *Education Week*, Nov. 1, 2007.

Pages 72–73: *In 2001, in Alexander v. Sandoval, the Supreme Court held that individuals no longer have the right to sue under Title VI of the Civil Rights Act* . . . see *Alexander v. Sandoval*, 532 U.S. 275 (2001).

Page 73: In 2009, *in Horne v. Flores, the Supreme Court held that, under the Equal Educational Opportunities Act* . . . see *Horne v. Flores*, 129 S.Ct. 2579 (2009).

Page 73: *In 2015, the Every Student Succeeds Act, which replaced the No Child Left Behind Act, was enacted by Congress* . . . see Every Student Succeeds Act, https://www.gpo.gov (search under "Every Student Succeeds Act," 114th Congress).

Chapter 7

Page 76: *Mary Beth Tinker was born in 1952 and grew up in Iowa . . . one of Mary Beth's early memories is of her parents going to Mississippi in 1964 . . . Mary Beth's teenage years coincided with the Vietnam War* . . . see "Mary Beth Tinker," Student Press Law Center, https://www.tinkertourusa.org.

Page 76: *In December 1965, a group of adults and students in Des Moines, including the Tinkers, attended a meeting at the home of Christopher Eckhardt . . . The principals of the Des Moines schools became aware of the plan . . . On December 16, Mary Beth Tinker and Christopher Eckhardt wore black armbands to their schools* . . . see facts described by the U.S. Supreme Court in *Tinker v. Des Moines Indep. Comm. Sch. Dist.*, 89 S.Ct. 733 (1968), 735.

Page 77: *Represented by the ACLU, the students and their families embarked* . . . see "Tinker v. Des Moines—Landmark Supreme Court Ruling on Behalf of Student Expression," American Civil Liberties Union, https://www.aclu.org.

Page 77: *On February 24, 1969, the U.S. Supreme Court reversed* . . . see *Tinker*, 89 S.Ct. at 739–41.

Page 77: Making History section . . . *Today, Mary Beth Tinker is an advocate for the rights of youth* . . . see "Mary Beth Tinker," Student Press Law Center, https://www.tinkertourusa.org.

Page 77: *She has observed a gradual erosion of free speech rights since 1969. "I think the political climate in the country discourages young people from speaking up" . . . "Without encouraging a climate where free speech and dissidents' voices flourish . . . we won't benefit as much as we could as a society"* . . . see "A Conversation with Mary Beth Tinker," American Bar Association, Aug. 29, 2017, https://www.americanbar.org.

Page 78: *The Decision* section generally . . . see *Tinker*, 89 S.Ct. at 736, 738.

Page 78: *Important Concepts* section . . . see *ibid.* at pp. 737–38, 740.

Page 78: *In Fact* section . . . see "Future of the First Amendment: 2016 Survey of High School Students and Teachers," Knight Foundation, Feb. 7, 2017, https://knight foundation.org.

Page 80: *General regulations involving appearance or dress codes have been upheld by courts* . . . see, for example, *Canady v. Bossier Parish School Board*, 240 F. 3d 437 (5th Cir. 2000).

Pages 83–84: *Recent Developments* section . . . see *Bethel Sch. Dist. No. 403 v. Fraser*, 106 S.Ct. 3159 (1986); *Hazelwood Sch. Dist. v. Kuhlmeier*, 108 S.Ct. 562 (1988); *Morse v. Frederick*, 127 S.Ct. 2618 (2007); *Bell v. Itawamba Ct. Sch. Bd.*, 799 F.3d 379 (5th Cir. 2015).

Chapter 8

Pages 86–87: *Years later, I learned that the New Jersey had passed a statute ostensibly to encourage "quiet and private contemplation and introspection"* . . . Stuart Taylor, Jr., "Moment of Silence Is Ended in Jersey," *New York Times*, Dec. 2, 1987.

Page 87: *Merith Weisman's graduation ceremony at Nathan Bishop Middle School was going smoothly* . . . see "To the Plaintiffs, A Prayer's a Prayer," *New York Times*, Mar. 19, 1991.

Page 87: *Public schools in Providence, Rhode Island had a policy to permit school principals to invite members of the clergy* . . . see U.S. Supreme Court opinion, *Lee v. Weisman*, 112 S.Ct. 2649 (1992), 2652.

Page 87: *Said father Daniel Weisman: "There was a benediction . . . I was totally disarmed, humiliated . . ." . . .* see "School Prayer: Lee v. Weisman," C-SPAN Interview, Nov. 4, 1991, https://www.c-span.org.

Page 87: *Daniel and Vivian Weisman called the school superintendent the next day . . .* see "To the Plaintiffs, A Prayer's a Prayer," *New York Times*.

Page 87: *Eventually, according to Daniel, a teacher on the faculty who was in charge with graduation found them with "good news" . . . We appreciated her gesture . . . we did not want to be the oppressors of other people, parading our religion out in public for other people to have to be consume . . ."* see "School Prayer: Lee v. Weisman," C-SPAN Interview.

Page 88: *The Weismans objected to the school principal, arguing that the rabbi's prayers could be offensive to some non-Jewish students . . . Vivian Weisman thought the school system was being insensitive to the diversity of the student body . . .* see "To the Plaintiffs, A Prayer's a Prayer," *New York Times*.

Page 88: *Daniel Weisman sought a temporary restraining order in the United States District Court . . .* see *Weisman*, 112 S.Ct. at 2653.

Page 88: *Rabbi Leslie Gutterman, of the Temple Beth-El in Providence, delivered the following invocation prayer . . . The Rabbi also led a benediction prayer . . .* see *Lee v. Weisman*, 112 S.Ct. 2649 (1992), at pp. 2652–53.

Page 89: *Making History* section generally . . . see Fox Butterfield, "Plaintiffs Are 'Thrilled' by School Prayer Ruling," *New York Times*, June 25, 1992.

Page 90: *The Case* section . . . see *Weisman*, 112 S.Ct. at 2661.

Pages 90–91: *The Decision* section . . . see *Weisman*, 112 S.Ct. at 2655, 2660–61.

Page 91: *The First Amendment of the U.S. Constitution states* . . . see U.S. Constitution, Amendment I, at https://www.law.cornell.edu (search under "Primary Sources: Constitution").

Page 91: *by the middle of the twentieth century, the First Amendment (and most of the Bill of Rights) had been interpreted to apply not just to the federal government but to state and local governments as well . . .* see, for example, *Everson v. Board of Education*, 330 U.S. 1 (1947) (holding that the First Amendment Establishment Clause applied to states).

Page 91: *As Justice Kennedy explained in the majority opinion, when the Constitution and Bill of Rights were being cobbled together . . .* see *Weisman*, 112 S.Ct. at 2656–57.

Page 92: *In a famous case*, Lemon v. Kurtzman . . . see *Lemon v. Kurtzman*, 403 U. S. 602 (1971).

Page 92: *In Fact* section . . . *In 1962, in* Engel v. Vitale, *for example, the Court invalidated a New York public school prayer . . . And in 1985 in* Wallace v. Jaffree, *the Court held that an Alabama statute authorizing a one-minute period of silence . . .* see *Engel* v. *Vitale*, 370 U. S. 421 (1962); *Wallace v. Jaffree*, 472 U.S. 38 (1985).

Pages 92–93: *The Court in* Weisman *appeared to address different parts of the* Lemon *test . . . But in reality the Court largely bypassed* Lemon *and focused instead on the coercive nature of school prayer . . .* see *Weisman*, 112 S.Ct. at 2655, 2659.

Page 93: *In* Board of Education v. Mergens . . . *The Court ruled similarly in the* Lamb's Chapel *and* Good News Club cases . . . see *Board of Education v. Mergens,* 496 U.S. 226 (1990); *Lamb's Chapel v. Center Moriches Union Free School District,* 508 U.S. 384 (1993); *Good News Club v. Milford Central School,* 533 U.S. 98 (2001).

Page 94: *I didn't support the 2002 ruling in* Zelman v. Simmons-Harris . . . see *Zelman v. Simmons-Harris,* 536 U.S. 639 (2002).

Page 96: *In 2000, in* Santa Fe Independent School District v. Doe . . . see *Santa Fe Indep. Sch. Dist. v. Doe,* 530 U.S. 290 (2000).

Page 97: *In 2018, Kentucky approved state academic standards for Bible literacy classes in public schools; the ACLU had voiced concern* . . . see Supriya Sridhar, "State Ed Board Approves Bible Literacy Standards for Public Schools," *Louisville Courier Journal,* June 7, 2018.

Page 97: *Also in 2018, a federal appellate court upheld a version of a student production of a "Christmas Spectacular"*. . . see *Freedom from Religion Foundation v. Concord Community Schools,* __ F.3d. __ (7th Cir. 2018).

Page 97: *The ACLU has represented several students in recent years who have been persecuted for expressing their religion at school* . . . see "ACLU Defense of Religious Practice and Expression in Public Schools," American Civil Liberties Union, https://www.aclu.org.

Chapter 9

Page 99: *In the 1980s, the focus was on deterring (and criminalizing) crack and cocaine use. In more recent years, the drug of choice has included heroin, methamphetamines, inhalants, and prescription medications* . . . see National Institute on Drug Abuse (search under "Trends and Statistics:"), https://www.drugabuse.gov.

Page 100: *In 2003, Savana Redding was an honor student in the eighth grade . . . Savana still remembers the clothes she had on—black stretch pants with butterfly patches and a pink T-shirt—the day school officials strip-searched her* . . . see Adam Liptak, "Strip Search of Girl Tests Limit of School Policy, *New York Times,* Mar. 23, 2009.

Page 100: *In October 2003, a Safford Middle School student named Jordan told school administrators that certain students were bringing drugs and weapons on campus . . . Wilson then called Marissa out of class . . . Wilson learned from staff members that Savana and Marissa were friends and were part of an "unusually rowdy group"* . . . see factual summary in the U.S. Supreme Court opinion, *Safford v. Redding,* 129 S.Ct. 2633 (2009), 2640–41.

Pages 100–101: *"I was in class, and the vice principal came, and got me out of class, and he started asking me some things . . . He asked me if he could search my backpack . . . We ended up in the nurse's office . . . I looked down, I didn't want to look at their faces, and I didn't want to cry"* . . . see "Strip-Search for Advil Case Before Supreme Court Today," Interview with Savana and April Redding, American Civil Liberties Union, Apr. 21, 2009, https://www.aclu.org.

Page 101: *After she had stripped to her underwear, "they asked me to pull out my bra and move it from side to side . . . They made me open my legs and pull out my underwear"* . . . see Liptak, "Strip Search of Girl Tests Limit of School Policy."

Page 101: *She says of the strip search: "[It] was the most humiliating experience I have ever had"* . . . see Bill Mears, "Teen Strip-Searched in School Wins Partial Victory," see *CNN,* June 25, 2009.

Page 101: *Savana was just told to go sit in the hallway for hours until school ended, and when he mother picked her up, Savana was "very withdrawn" and crying* . . . see *ibid.*

Page 101: *The experience left her wary, nervous and distrustful, and she developed bleeding stomach ulcers* . . . see Liptak, "Strip Search of Girl Tests Limit of School Policy."

Page 101: *Her mother, April Redding, disagreed. "They changed my kid, and they need to understand what they took away from her"* . . . see "Student Strip Search Heads to High Court," *CBS News*, Apr. 20, 2009.

Page 101: *"Before it happened, I loved school, loved everything about it. You know, I had a 4.0 GPA, honor roll, and now, well, afterwards I never wanted to go to school again"* . . . see Mears, "Teen Strip-Searched in School Wins Partial Victory."

Page 102: *The Case section* . . . see *Redding*, 129 S.Ct. at 2643.

Page 102: *The Decision section* . . . see *Redding*, 129 S.Ct. at 2641, 2643.

Page 103: *Making History section* . . . *Some years after the* Safford *case had been decided, Justice Ruth Bader Ginsburg recalled how* . . . see Linda Hirshman, "What's the Difference?: How Sandra Day O'Connor, Ruth Bader Ginsburg, and Sonia Sotomayor Brought Wisdom to the Supreme Court," *Slate*, Aug. 25, 2015.

Page 103: *I would like for every parent in the United States to understand the authority that we have given schools," she said* . . . see "Strip-Search for Advil Case Before Supreme Court Today," Interview with Savana and April Redding, American Civil Liberties Union, Apr. 21, 2009, https://www.aclu.org.

Page 103: *"I am excited that [the Court] agreed with me, they see that it was wrong for the school to do that"* . . . see Bill Mears, "Teen Strip-Searched in School Wins Partial Victory," see *CNN*, June 25, 2009.

Page 103: *"What they did was wrong, and they feel like they didn't do anything wrong, and that really hurts, but it's more about other kids"* . . . see "Strip-Search for Advil Case Before Supreme Court Today," Interview with Savana and April Redding, American Civil Liberties Union, Apr. 21, 2009, https://www.aclu.org.

Page 103: *She said the long legal battle "was to make sure it didn't happen to anyone else"* . . . see Robert Barnes, "Supreme Court Rules Strip Search Violated 13-Year-Old Girl's Rights," *Washington Post*, June 26, 2009.

Page 104: *But the Supreme Court held in 1985 in the* New Jersey v. T. L. O. *case* . . . see *New Jersey v. T. L. O.*, 469 U.S. 325 (1985).

Page 104: *reasonable grounds for suspecting that the search will turn up evidence* . . . *reasonably related in scope to the circumstances which justified the interference in the first place* . . . see *Redding*, 129 S.Ct. at 2642, 2647.

Page 105: *In Fact section* . . . see *T. L. O.*, 469 U.S. at 325; *Vernonia Sch. Dist. 47J v. Acton*, 515 U.S. 646 (1995), *Board of Educ. Of Indep. Sch. Dist. No. 92 v. Earls*, 536 U.S. 822 (2002).

Page 105: *note that courts have generally upheld the use of walk-through and hand-held metal detectors in schools* . . . see "Metal Detectors in Schools," Texas Association of School Boards, Feb. 2019, https://www.tasb.org; *In re Latasha W.*, 60 Cal.App.4th 1524 (1998).

Page 105: *Notably, as of 2018, while student drug use (other than marijuana) is at its lowest levels in over two decades* . . . see "Monitoring the Future Survey: High School and Youth Trends," National Institute on Drug Abuse, Dec. 2018, https://www.drugabuse.gov.

Page 105: *K–12 school shooting incidents and deaths are at their highest levels in history* . . . see "K–12 School Shooting Database," Center for Homeland Defense and Security, https://www.chds.us.

Pages 109–110: *Recent Developments* section . . . see *D.H. by Dawson v. Clayton County School District*, 830 F.3d 1306 (11th Cir. 2016); *A.M. v. Holmes*, 830 F.3d 1123 (10th Cir. 2016); *Jackson v. Ladner*, 626 F. Appx. 80 (5th Cir. 2015).

Page 110: *In the last several years, however, the Supreme Court has acted to limit the government's access to individuals' digital information* . . . see *Carpenter v. United States*, 585 U.S. __ (2018); *Riley v. California*, 134 S.Ct. 2473 (2014).

Chapter 10

Page 112: *In the spring of 1971, during a period of heightened racial consciousness* . . . see Appellees' Brief on the Merits, *Goss v. Lopez*, 1974 WL 185915, No. 73-898, May 29, 1974.

Page 113: *Tension had mounted at Central High School during Black History Week* . . . see *Lopez v. Williams*, 372 F. Supp. 1279, (S.D. Ohio 1973), 1285.

Page 113: *while Dwight was in the lunchroom, students came in and started overturning tables . . . On March 8, Dwight went with his mother and a sister to the disciplinary meeting, but the entrance of the building was blocked . . . Dwight was transferred from Central High School to the Adult Day School* . . . see Appellees' Brief on the Merits, 1974 WL 185915.

Pages 113–114: *He later testified that at least seventy-five other students were suspended from his school. He eventually joined eight other students* . . . see *ibid.*

Page 114: *The students also argued that no hearing or conference designed to elicit the truth was conducted* . . . see *Lopez v. Williams*, 372 F. Supp. at 1281–92.

Page 114: *On January 22, 1975, the U.S. Supreme Court invalidated the suspensions of Dwight and other students* . . . see *Lopez*, 419 U.S. at 581–82.

Page 114: *The Decision* section . . . see *Lopez*, 419 U.S. at 574, 581, 584.

Pages 115–116: *Making History* section generally . . . see Thomas J. Flygare, "Ten Years After Goss v. Lopez: An Interview with Peter D. Roos," *Phi Delta Kappan*, Vol. 66, No. 6, Feb.1985, 441–442.

Page 116, 118: *Important Concepts* section . . . see *Lopez*, 419 U.S. at 582–84.

Page 117: *In Fact* section . . . *In July 1969, riots and fire bombings were sparked by the killing of a black father by a white dry cleaner on Columbus' Near East Side* . . . see M. Ferenchik, "Scars Remain 40 Years After Near East Side Riot," *Columbus Dispatch*, July 21, 2009.

Page 117: *In January 1970, the murder of a black man by a white police officer known as "Machine Gun Morgan" sparked racial tension* . . . see G. Tebben, "Columbus Mileposts: March 10, 1971: 'Machine Gun Morgan' acquitted," *Columbus Dispatch*, Mar. 10, 2012.

Page 117: *College campuses in Ohio and nationwide were hotbeds of protest in the early 1970s . . . In May 1970, National Guardsmen shot and killed four students at Ohio's Kent State University during Vietnam-Era protests* . . . see L. Hallow and D. Tussel, "1970 Protests Erupted Across Ohio, Tear Gas at OSU," *The Lantern*, May 3, 2010.

Page 117: *During this period, some estimate that half the country's student population were taking part in anti-war activities* . . . see L.A. Kauffman, *Direct Action: Protest and the Reinvention of American Radicalism* (Verso Books, 2017).